Second Chance

Second Chance

R. T. KENDALL

HODDER

British Library Cataloguing in Publication Data
A record for this book is available from the British Library

ISBN 978 0340 95492 8

Typeset in SabonMT by Avon DataSet Ltd, Bidford on Avon, Warwickshire

Printed and bound in Great Britain by
Clays Ltd, St Ives plc

Hodder & Stoughton
A division of Hachette Livre UK Ltd
338 Euston Road
London NW1 3BH
www.madaboutbooks.com

To all who need a Second Chance

Contents

Forewords   IX

Introduction   XVII

1   God's House   I
2   Ending Well   17
3   God's Blueprint   32
4   The Quality of the Superstructure   47
5   Money and Sex   66
6   Power   94
7   The Mighty Fallen   113
8   The Returning Backslider   142
9   Repentance   165
10   Simon Peter   186

Conclusion   210
Sample chapter of R.T. Kendall's   213
Totally Forgiving Ourselves

Foreword by Dr Jack Deere

Can the fallen be restored? We know they can because the apostle Paul wrote, 'Brothers, if someone is caught in a sin, you who are spiritual should restore him gently. But watch yourself, or you also may be tempted' (Gal. 6:1). And this is good news, because as R.T. suggests, who among us hasn't fallen to one degree or another? Yet restoration seems to be one of the ministries that the church does not do very well. For example, people overtaken by an addiction – it may be a sexual addiction or a chemical addiction – usually end up going outside the church for help. There are, of course, Christian recovery groups within the church. But when they offer an annual conference, maybe 200 people show up. When Alcoholics Anonymous host their annual conference, more than 70,000 people show up. Who would have ever thought the church, with all its emphasis on the grace and power of God, would be so inept at leading alcoholics to restoration? Who would have ever thought that a group of recovering alcoholics referring to God as 'your higher power' would do so much better at getting and keeping people sober?

After my church member attended her first AA meeting, she said to me, 'I wish the church could be more like that.'

'What do you mean?' I asked.

'Well, everyone was so real, and there was no judgement.'

This is what every church member says after their first AA meeting. I've heard it many times now. And these words take us right back to Paul's words in Galatians 6:1. He said that the '*spiritual*' should do the restoring. But who are the spiritual? At a minimum, the spiritual ones are those who can restore the fallen *gently*. We can't restore the fallen gently if we are judging them at the same time. Jesus told us that would be like trying to take a speck out of someone's eye while we have a plank in our own eye (Matt. 7:1–5). To judge someone in this sense means that we feel superior to them, and when we feel superior to someone, we never fail to communicate that feeling. Who of us enjoys being around people who feel superior to us? Perhaps we have so little restoration in the church because we have so much judgement in the church.

'Everyone was so real,' she said. I am haunted by those words these days. In the church the alternative to being real is being religious. Christ rescued me from an early and reckless death at 17. My early Christian experience was real because my mentors were spiritual men. They were leaders in the youth parachurch movement called Young Life. I could talk to them about anything without fear of losing their respect or affection. I knew I would get the help I needed. And a young man being inundated with ever increasing waves of testosterone needs a lot of help.

I finished college and got a new set of mentors, seminary professors. In my first few months at seminary, I had lunch with one of my professors. I was telling him about a sexual struggle I had had with my college girlfriend. I saw the pained look on his face as he changed the conversation to a benign subject. I thought, *Note to self, Jack, this is not an acceptable topic around here.* So I started working on my image. One of the things I learned in seminary and my subsequent church experience was that I needed to appear better than I was. I wish someone had told me that image management requires us to spend so much time both rehearsing and being on stage that there is very little time left over for real living. Religious people are actors and judges. They are not restorers.

People raised in a religious environment don't usually make very good candidates for restoration when they fall. They have been taught for so long to go underground with their sin that the light hurts their eyes too much. They don't realise how quickly the pain would pass if they would just walk out into the light all at once. But their devotion to the *image* of a holy person who has never existed holds them back. They have trusted that image to protect them rather than trusting the only true Protector. And they have seen what the judges did to others who fell.

What do you say to a person like this? How do you know if they have repented? How do you know if you have repented? What are some of the most common traps that cause people to fall? What is lost when we fall? R.T. Kendall addresses these questions and many more. He writes with the clarity and simplicity of one who understands both the Scriptures and history. This is the best book I've read on restoration. We need this book because we need to get better at restoration.

R.T. points out that even the righteous fall. Look at King David. But when the righteous fall, they rise again (Prov. 24:16). The story of the prodigal son teaches us that our rising is more pleasing to our Father than our fall is displeasing. Perhaps if the church really believed this we'd see a lot less falling and a lot more restoring.

Dr Jack Deere

Foreword by Dr Michael Eaton

Considered at any level, this is one of R.T.'s greatest books. It might turn out to be the most important. For the backslider it will bring great encouragement. For every Christian it will inspire each of us to strive for high levels of love and purity. It gives much needed help and advice concerning our sexuality, our handling of money and power, our need to stay confident and careful at the same time. For myself I know of no book that is so deeply challenging in its call to the life of wholesomeness and holiness, yet it is without the 'heaviness' and even oppressiveness that we associate with such themes.

But in addition to its inspirational practicality, R.T. Kendall's work on the restoration of morally fallen Christians is an important work for other reasons, more so than one might perhaps think at first glance. The fourth century in the church was famous for establishing the deity of Christ; Athanasius was the great name. The early fifth century was notable for clarifying the grace of God. We think in this connection of Augustine of Hippo and his work. Anselm in the tenth century made some improvements in the doctrine of the atonement. Luther brought to light justification by faith as never before. William Carey and Hudson Taylor were major thinkers behind the missionary movement. But the question we might want to ask is: when the history of the late twentieth and early twenty-first centuries are written (assuming the world survives long enough), what progress of doctrine will we associate with the period we are currently living in? Some of the answers to this question are already becoming clear. It has been a time when the **experiential** workings of the Spirit have been discussed more than ever. Calvin was clear and strong on the secret workings of the Spirit; the Pentecostal and charismatic movements have driven us to consider the more experiential work of the Spirit, to which Calvin gave little thought. Massive church growth has taken place in areas of the church where evangelicals have accepted these doctrinal developments.

But there is another answer to our question. The period we are living in will surely become known as the time when the relationship and clear distinctiveness of justification over against 'inheritance' and 'reward' is being clarified as never before. Suppose reward and justification are distinct, and suppose the great warnings of the Bible (notably the series in Hebrews 2:1–4: 3:7–4:13; 6:3–12; 10:26–39; 12:15–17, 25) are about reward and **not** about our unshakable 'eternal redemption' mentioned in Hebrews 9:12 or our being 'perfected for all time' as we have it in Hebrews 10:14. Suppose Hebrews 10 refers to **reward** when it says 'If we go on sinning deliberately after receiving the knowledge of the truth, there no longer remains a sacrifice for sins, but a fearful expectation of judgment . . .' (10:26, 27). Suppose Hebrews 10:35 is simply continuing the theme when it says 'Do not throw away your confident faith; it has a great **reward**' (Hebrews 10:35). Then the way has been opened for a great and powerful doctrine of eternal security plus an immensely significant and forceful doctrine of loss and reward for the saved at the judgement seat of Christ.

This is the major forward step in theological thinking in the late twentieth century, done not so much by professors in universities or seminaries as by preachers leading churches who seek to motivate and inspire their people. There were many forerunners to this style of thinking and a scholar studying at doctoral level could a long time ago insist that 'Luther's unambiguous rejection of the doctrine of **merit** must not deceive us into thinking that the Reformer does not hold fast to the biblical sayings about reward' (Johann Heinz, *Justification and Merit*, Andrews University Press, 1984, pp. 217–218). According to Luther, merit-morality (*der schendliche Tück*) seeks its own honour, but the biblical reward-teaching is different! It is full of grace. It allows for no pride. It makes us long to stretch forward to high levels of humble achievement in the kingdom of God. The modern forward-step – increasingly being realised – of distinguishing justification and inheritance – is only a small development of what has been Protestant teaching all along.

The next question to be considered is: how should this be preached? What is the practical outworking of this for the life of the churches? How should we **preach** reward and the fear (amidst exuberant assurance of salvation) of displeasing God? How can we **preach** judgement day **without** saying to our people 'You are maybe not "saved" after all'? It is at this point that R.T.'s work is outstanding. There is a biblical doctrine of assurance. It is staggering in its power. It will lift us up to heaven. But there is also a fearful warning to any who wish to persist in extreme rebelliousness. It combines amazing encouragements for the scandalous backslider but fearful warnings of disgrace if rebellion continues. It is at this point we have R.T.'s major contribution to the churches. Here we have a style of thinking and preaching that motivates us with ecstatic joy – and yet puts some sobriety in us at the same time. Here is 'the fear of the Lord' without the endless doubts and trouble of conscience that beset any who 'go about to establish their own righteousness'. Here is theology on fire, theology at its best, theology that rescues the fallen. We might need it sooner than we think.

Dr Michael Eaton
Nairobi, Kenya

Introduction

When Oliver Cromwell (1599–1658), often known as the 'Lord Protector' of England, viewed the portrait for which he had posed, he was offended. His face was seen with a perfect complexion, much like a modern photograph. 'Where are the warts?' he asked. The reply was that the artist had removed them. Cromwell demanded that the portrait be repainted and presented to history 'warts and all'.

That is the way the Bible presents its heroes. The history of the Christian Church is full of stories of people who have been truly converted, but have grievously fallen. The same is true of the Old Testament. Unlike most modern biographies, the authors of Scripture present its heroes with 'warts and all'.

This book will have a good deal to say about the Judgement Seat of Christ. In a word, all *Christians* will face judgement – standing before the Lord Jesus Christ, 'that each one may receive what is due to him for the things

done while in the body, whether good or bad' (2 Cor. 5:10).
I will unpack this neglected teaching later on.

I remember having a long discussion with Arthur Blessitt
in London when I was the Minister of Westminster Chapel.
The issue was this: will *all* that is knowable about us be
revealed to everybody at the Judgement Seat of Christ?
Arthur believes that *everything* – even our sins – will be
revealed. 'But what about the sins that have been washed
away by the blood of Christ?' I probed. Arthur replied that
even King David's sins were revealed – along with others in
the Bible, all of whom were clearly saved people. Arthur
then asked, 'Why would everything be revealed that David
did, but we get away with the things we have done?' Arthur
reckoned that, as the Bible told the truth about Moses,
Abraham, Jacob, David, Jonah and others – hiding nothing
– so too will all be revealed about us.

I hope Arthur is wrong. I, for one, would not want you
to find out all that is knowable about *me* at the Judgement
Seat of Christ. Furthermore, I could easily make a good
case against this unusual and sobering point of view. But
Arthur believes that it will be the revelation of *everything*
that *all of us have done* that will bring weeping at the
Judgement Seat of Christ. 'Why would there be tears at the
Judgement if we are going to heaven?', Arthur asked. He
added, 'God will say, "This is what you did but you are
forgiven", and this is when God will wipe away all our
tears' (Rev. 21:4).

Why is it that *some* Christians are exposed and judged in

the here and now but others are not, although the latter have done things that are equally scandalous and heinous in God's eyes? For those of us who have not been caught (but who have made the angels blush nevertheless), is it because we are more godly, more worthy, more valuable or more special than those who were found out? If God judged the only person described in Scripture as the man after his own heart (1 Sam. 13:14; Acts 13:22), why do you think he would not judge you and me?

Tell me, have you not thought about this issue before?

When Paul said, 'Knowing the terror of the Lord, we persuade men' (AV), it followed his statement: 'For we must all appear before the judgment seat of Christ, that each one may receive what is due to him for the things done while in the body, whether good or bad' (2 Cor. 5:10–11). This is clearly a reference to Christians, and is enough to scare us to death.

Martin Luther (1483–1546) said he expected three surprises when he got to heaven: (1) there will be those there he did not think would be there; (2) there would be those missing he was sure would be there; and (3) that he were there himself!

If I could borrow from Luther's observation, I too expect three surprises at the Judgement Seat of Christ: (1) there will be those who receive a reward that I did not think would get it; (2) there will be those who are *passed over* for a reward that I thought surely would receive it; and (3) that I myself would receive a reward.

I have already written a book called the *Judgment Seat of Christ* (Christian Focus Publications, originally published as *When God Says 'Well Done'*), so I will not repeat all that is found there. But this book will none the less focus on certain principles in the New Testament about preparation for the Final Judgement, especially looking at Paul's views in 1 Corinthians 3. But why should I bring in the Judgement Seat of Christ at all? It is because the lack of appropriate preparation for the Final Judgement can result in God stepping in now – and judging those who did not take this preparation seriously.

I hold that there are two phases of the Judgement Seat of Christ: (1) when God separates the saved from the lost – the saved go to heaven and the lost go to hell; (2) when God calls every single Christian who ever lived to give an account of the things done in the body, whether 'good or bad' – some receiving a reward, others being saved by 'fire' with no reward, as we will see below.

In summary, God will judge *all* of us on the 'final day' at the Judgement, but for some reason he chooses to judge only *some* of us on this present pilgrimage on our way to that Day.

It is hard to imagine *anybody* who can anticipate the Judgement Seat of Christ with glee and excitement. It surely will be a thousand times worse than waiting for the outcome of a verdict or an examination here on earth.

But because John talked about having boldness or 'confidence on the day of judgment' (1 John 4:17) and being 'unashamed before him at his coming' (1 John 2:28), I now breathe a sigh of great relief. I infer from these verses that, since my sins have been purified by the blood of Christ, *truly buried* in the depths of the sea (Micah 7:19), *not remembered* (Heb. 8:12), and separated from us 'as far as the east is from the west' (Ps. 103:12), you will not find out on that Day all that could be known of me.

And yet this matter of standing before God Almighty at the Judgement Seat to give an account of the things done in the body – 'whether good or bad' – is still enough to send shivers down the spine of every soul. I simply do not want *you* to know what I know about me. I am counting on the blood of Jesus shielding you from the knowledge of what my sins were – not to mention God screening my family, my friends and those to whom I have ministered over the last fifty years – and from knowing the total truth of all that God graciously forgave me of.

As to why some people are judged in the here and now and others are not, I conclude two things: first, the answer resides partly in these words: 'I will have mercy on whom I will have mercy' (Exod. 33:19). It therefore lies in the mystery of God's inscrutable sovereignty. You and I should never forget this. Don't fancy yourself as being clever – or very important to God – if you don't get caught. That is foolish thinking. But, second, know also that nothing happens without a reason. God has a purpose in everything he does, doesn't do, or permits. If God rolls up his sleeves and openly judges one of his children in the present era, there is a good reason for it. After all, to those who love God, being called according to his purpose, there is a wonderful, wonderful promise: all things work together for good (Rom. 8:28).

There are perhaps three categories of people reading this book: (1) you have never grievously fallen, but fully realise your capabilities and know God to be merciful to you by dealing with you secretly by the internal chastening of the Holy Spirit, and therefore you have not (so far) given in to temptation; (2) you have indeed, sadly, succumbed to temptation – whether it be with regard to bitterness, self-vindication, damaging another's reputation, worldly things, money, sex or power – but you have not been openly exposed (up to now); and (3) you gave in to one or more of these temptations but also got caught – and have been openly judged by the Lord so that your reputation has been hurt and your ministry, career or position in the Church has been, at least for a while, put in abeyance.

It is impossible to say which one of these three categories of people needs this book most, but I am mainly addressing category (3): Christians, including those in the ministry, who have fallen *and* were found out.

If you are reading this and have been exposed, and have lost either your ministry or your reputation, how do you feel? Are you bitter that you got caught? Do you feel it was unfair that someone 'blew the whistle' on you? Do you feel that God has been unfair? Do you feel that the people who accused *you* also have skeletons in *their* wardrobes, and that it is grossly unfair that *they* are the ones who have pointed the finger? Or are you angry that there are others who have done the same thing as you – or even worse things – but have continued in their jobs or ministry without any fear?

So, I would lovingly ask you, how do *you* feel that you have been openly judged?

I am reminded of a story that my friend Rob Parsons shared with me. One Sunday morning, during one of the darkest hours of his life, the well-known British preacher David Pawson unexpectedly knocked on Rob's door. David began speaking to Rob about how painful he found it to be aware that Rob was the subject of rumours. But God spoke to David Pawson and said, 'I know the *whole* truth, and the truth is worse than what they know; and I still love you.' Then David Pawson gave Rob these words: 'This too will pass, and the truth is worse than what they know.' The comforting thought that *this too will pass* means that the immediate crisis will not last for ever; God knows how much we can bear, and he has a way of enabling us to move on and then watch *him* cause everything to work together for good (Rom. 8:28).

I say to every reader, whoever you are, in whatever category you may be: the present situation will pass. And the truth is even less palatable than what people already know. But that things are not even worse than they are is owing to the sheer grace and mercy of God.

I do know of one church leader who was recently

exposed who said that he was *glad* – that he thanked God for it. The exposure led to his repentance, so you could argue that it is God himself showing sovereign mercy in exposing us, however painful that will be.

However, this book is certainly not just for those in ministry. If you are what might be called a 'layperson' – a Christian in business, or have a secular job in a worldly environment – this book is just as much for you. The only difference is that the situation of a layperson being exposed (unless he or she happens to have a very high profile in the church or community) tends to receive less attention than a scandal involving a minister within the Church.

So, if you feel I have described you in any way in these previous paragraphs, I plead with you to walk with me through this book. I say this because you, like all of us, have to stand before God at the Judgement Seat of Christ to receive a reward for things done in the body, whether 'good or bad'.

We have all sinned to some degree on a scale from 1 (minor – as in thoughts or words) to 10 (major – as in thoughts, words and scandalous deeds). Some argue that 'sin is sin' and that in the sight of God it doesn't matter how serious the sin is. This is not true. Some sins *are* worse than others. This is revealed by the various punishments for sin meted out by the Mosaic Law (see especially Leviticus and Deuteronomy), not to mention that Jesus himself talked about the 'greater sin' (John 19:11) and stated that the punishment for some will be more severe than for others (Luke 12:47–48). Some sins therefore bring greater dishonour to the name of our Most Holy God and are judged accordingly.

My first ever published book was on Jonah and I had chosen the book of Jonah for my first series of sermons at Westminster Chapel in 1977. People asked me why. I had one answer: 'I am Jonah; I know what it is to be found out.' It was why I felt I could preach from that book.

Have you ever been found out?

I have had the privilege of knowing a good number of great and famous men and women – church leaders and heads of state – and a few of them I got to know rather well. I learned a number of things, but one was (without exception) that those people I began to admire a little bit too much sooner or later disappointed me. The more I had admired them, the greater the devastation when they let me down. A book I will never write could be entitled *Great Men Who Disappointed Me and Why*! I pray nobody will write such a book and include me, though there are those out there who could easily do this! If people have let me down, I certainly know that I have let others down too.

My point is this. I do not write this book sitting on a high pedestal looking down at you. In fact, the truth is I write this book with fear and trembling.

The purpose of these pages is partly to caution you if you have *not* fallen – lest you become self-righteous and think it can't happen to you.

I write also, as lovingly as I know how, to urge you if you *have* fallen, but have not yet been judged for it, to come to an unfeigned repentance.

But I write mainly to encourage you if you have fallen, publicly or privately – especially if you fear you cannot be fully restored or used by God again. There will be some hard issues and passages of Scripture to face, and we will call a spade a spade. But to those who can 'hear his voice' (Heb. 3:7), I give you the categorical assurance that you *can* be used again – just like David and others in the Bible who fell from grace but were restored by God.

1

God's House

. . . you are God's field, God's building.

(1 Cor. 3:9)

And we are his house, if we hold on to our
courage and the hope of which we boast.

(Heb. 3:6)

In a large house there are articles not only of
gold and silver, but also of wood and clay; some
are for noble purposes and some for ignoble. If
a man cleanses himself from the latter, he will
be an instrument for noble purposes, made holy,
useful to the Master and prepared to do any
good work. (2 Tim. 2:20–21)

The price of greatness is responsibility.

Winston Churchill

I don't usually remember the exact time or place when bad news comes my way. But I do remember exactly where I was at 11.45 a.m. on 9 October 2004 – in the Dallas-Fort Worth airport on our way to El Dorado, Arkansas – when my friend Jack Taylor soberly relayed the news to me that our highly esteemed friend, who was a well-known preacher, famed for his extraordinary prophetic gift, had just been found guilty of homosexual sin. I was stunned and in shock for weeks. Although I had assumed I was one of his closest friends, I never suspected or dreamed that he could be doing anything like that.

If *you* are one who has fallen, you no doubt dreaded that others would hear what it was that you did. You would have thought about those who have admired you. You perhaps thought of those who were your personal enemies – who, sadly, might rejoice at your downfall. You would have thought also about how hurt and shocked those close to you would be. Part of the pain of getting caught is the fear that people who never suspected your weakness would be disillusioned – not only with you, but with the gospel you have upheld.

Do you know what it is like to have such high esteem for someone – and then have that person let you down? Can you imagine how the angels in heaven feel when the name of God is brought into disrepute by a scandal involving Christians?

'The price of greatness is responsibility,' said Winston Churchill, and the higher one's profile in the Church, the greater the responsibility that person has to maintain a godly walk. 'Not many of you should presume to be teachers, my brothers, because you know that we who teach will be judged more strictly' (James 3:1).

As I said above, I envisage three categories of people reading this book, but I will mainly keep in mind the person who has *already* fallen – and fears he or she cannot be used by God again. If this applies to you, I can understand that you might want to jump ahead and read those chapters that you think are more relevant to you. However, I would urge you not to do that, but to read line by line what I have to say. Here is why: those who do not learn from their past mistakes are doomed to repeat them. It is essential that you learn not only *what* went wrong – but *why*. Everything I write here is designed not only to give you hope for a brilliant future, but to ensure you do not fall again. It has everything to do with building a solid superstructure on the right foundation.

The church of which I was a part as I grew up in Ashland, Kentucky, always had twelve-day 'revivals' three times every year – autumn, winter and spring. I myself had to be in church every single night of each one of them. But they shaped my life and ministry and I now thank God for those days. The best evangelists and preachers of my old denomination (Church of the Nazarene) were brought in. In my mind these people were all on a pedestal – and most of them deserved that admiration.

But I will never forget how I heard that one of them –

possibly my favourite evangelist as I grew up – had been living in sexual immorality for years, even at the same time as he was ministering to our church. It was revealed that a woman followed him wherever he went and managed to stay in the same hotel in which he was booked. What is more, he preached with as much power as I had ever witnessed. The way he could move people was amazing. A sense of the fear of God fell on the crowds as he spoke. He had such descriptive powers with language that when he preached on the subject of everlasting hell, for example, you could almost smell the brimstone. Dozens came forward night after night to be saved. There is no doubt that God used that man with many people, including me.

At the age of nineteen I first became a pastor of a church in Palmer, Tennessee. The district superintendent who put me there was one of my heroes. One Sunday morning in the spring of 1956 he turned up unexpectedly at my church. I was thrilled and asked him to preach. During his sermon I had a vision – there to my astonishment was the Lord Jesus looking directly at him with utter disapproval. I could not understand it. I could not deny the vision, but it did not tally with what I knew about him. I never told anybody about this. What is more, I had to wait a long time to understand it. Ten years later it was revealed that he had been involved in an affair with a woman in Chattanooga, and was forced to resign as district superintendent. That affair was apparently going on when he preached for me.

People ask: 'How can a person's gift flourish when they are living in sin?' I can only answer with Romans 11:29: 'For God's gifts and his call are irrevocable'; 'God does not change his mind about whom he chooses and blesses' (Today's English Version); 'God does not withdraw his gifts or calling' (New English Bible). The Greek actually uses *ametameleta* – literally, God's gifts and calling are 'without repentance' (as in the AV). This verse refers principally to God's own decree – that God will not change his mind; but Paul is also saying that whether or not a person has repented of his or her sins is *not a necessary condition* for receiving or maintaining a spiritual gift.

Spiritual or ministerial gifts are sovereignly bestowed on a person – not because of one's good works or sanctification. This explains how King Saul – whom God had chosen but later had clearly rejected (1 Sam. 10:1, 16:1, 18:12) – still prophesied. Saul had been given a change of heart along with the gift of prophecy (1 Sam. 10:9–10). But later, strange as it may seem, *on his way to kill young David*, 'the Spirit of God came upon him' and the people were still saying, 'Is Saul also among the prophets?' (1 Sam. 19:23–24; cf. 1 Sam. 10:11). God's approval had been withdrawn, but not Saul's gift.

Saul's example also explains how the aforementioned evangelist I admired, as well as my old district superintendent, could preach with effectiveness and yet be so hypocritical. This of course provides a theological rationale as to how the fallen TV evangelists in the 1980s could carry on in their private lives without pure hearts and yet mesmerise their followers – and even be used of God.

But having an irrevocable gift does not mean that one is exempt from God's severe displeasure and judgement. A gift from God is bestowed upon the assumption that one will not abuse such a privilege. That person should be utterly grateful to God for his or her talent, anointing, natural ability, and his or her calling and following. If the person is not full of gratitude – which is demonstrated by words and deeds – then he or she will sooner or later be found out, and will also discover that the effectiveness of that gift diminishes.

As for King Saul, he eventually lost everything – including any connection with anything prophetic. 'God has turned away from me. He no longer answers me, either by prophets or by dreams', lamented Saul near the end of his life (1 Sam. 28:15). I would suspect therefore that a person's gift can flourish for a while despite his or her conduct, but that eventually that gift will begin to disappear if the person is not finally granted unfeigned repentance. Therefore the irrevocability of one's gift should not be regarded as meaning that it will be *effective* for ever.

As a matter of fact, when I reflected on the afore-mentioned fallen preacher with the unusual prophetic gift, I realised he had begun to prophesy with less and less accuracy – regarding both past, present and future events.

Whereas he was once known to have 100 per cent accuracy (John Wimber personally told me he never knew this man to get it wrong), that began to change at some point. He began to get it wrong. For example, during one of my last visits to him he emphatically stated to me that George W. Bush would be a 'one-term president' – but Bush was in fact re-elected. That was a pretty big 'miss'. I am therefore saying that a person's gift may flourish for a while when they are living in sin, but not be effective for ever.

Judgement on God's house

Why does God step in and judge some, but leave others to continue in their sin? The answer is that it has mostly to do with God's sovereign and inscrutable purposes, but also his infinite patience. And yet it may also have something to do with how angry God is, in which case he may prefer to wait and deal with some disobedient servants at the Final Judgement. However, all sin will be judged sooner or later – whether in this life or at the Judgement Seat of Christ.

The Apostle Peter stated that judgement 'must begin at the house of God' (1 Pet. 4:17 – AV; the word 'family' is used instead of 'house' in the NIV). This is because God has chosen to delay judging the world generally until he has first called his own people to give an account regarding their covenant responsibility. He therefore starts the process of judgement with his elect people first.

He often begins with those in leadership. Why? Because leaders are supposed to *lead* – not follow – by a higher level of wisdom and also by example. They are not to be, as it was once said, 'Like people, like priests' (Hos. 4:9), in that the priests mirrored the people's unjust wishes and ungodly example. Leaders were to be different. *Like priest, like people*. This assumes the priest is of impeccable integrity, character and reputation – the way it should be.

But when leaders go wrong, the people go wrong. It filters from the top downwards. When leaders do not uphold God's standard, the people will not have a sense of direction. God judged Eli, the high priest, before he judged the people of Israel generally (1 Sam. 4). Moreover, as I stated, those who are teachers – or leaders – will be judged more strictly (James 3:1).

When Peter said that judgement must begin with the house, or family, of God I don't think he was referring to an order of events at the Final Judgement, although it could imply that. If so, it could therefore suggest that the *saved* will be dealt with before the lost are held accountable at the Final Judgement. However, I think Peter's statement that judgement must begin with the family of God refers to the way that God has chosen to deal with his own people in the here and now – in advance of the Final Judgement.

We must never forget this incontrovertible fact: we are *all* going to face God's Final Judgement. We should live our lives accordingly. That is one of the reasons that the Bible tells us there is a coming Judgement – to change our lives *now* and to prepare us for that frightening Event.

But it is equally true that God can give us a taste of the Final Judgement – in advance of that Day. As a matter of fact, good preaching on the subject of the Final Judgement should do this. When the reality of eternity is brought home so that it invades the present, the people will sense the fear of God and even feel something of what it will be like on that Day.

And yet a foretaste of the Final Judgement is what is actually taking place when you read of certain people who have been 'caught'. People like this who are being exposed is no accident; it is what *God* does. It is judgement in advance of the Judgement. When Paul says that if we judge ourselves, we will not be judged (1 Cor. 11:31), referring to the Lord's Supper, he is telling us that you and I can be spared this judgement below – and the full effects of the Final Judgement – if we deal with sin in the here and now. Dealing with our sin in the here and now means (1) acknowledging it, not denying it; and (2) repenting of it.

It could be more painful to be found out *then* – at the Judgement Seat of Christ – than to be exposed *now* in advance of the Judgement. There is an observable pattern in the history of God's dealings with his people: the angrier God is, the longer he sometimes waits before showing his ire. However painful it must be to be caught and judged here below, it will be worse at the Judgement Seat.

Uses of 'house' in Scripture

As we noted earlier, the Greek word *oikou* – 'house' in 1 Peter 4:17 (AV) – is translated 'family' of God in the New International Version. The word 'house' is used in multitudinous ways in the Bible. For example, it may refer to a physical structure (or superstructure above a foundation); it may refer to God's manifest presence; or it may refer to people. The first time the word 'house' occurs in the Bible is when God said to Noah, 'Come thou and all thy house into the ark' (Gen. 7:1 – AV; translated 'family' in the NIV).

The first time the phrase 'house of God' occurs in the Bible is when Jacob woke up after his dream of the angels and said, 'Surely the Lord is in this place, and I was not aware of it . . . How awesome is this place! This is none other than the house of God; this is the gate of heaven' (Gen. 28:16–17).

I have been amazed to see how vast the subject of 'house' is in the Bible. The word itself appears no fewer than 2,000 times – but used, as I have said, in many different ways. 'House' therefore can refer not only to people or a building, but also to the temple: 'My house will be called a house of prayer' (Matt. 21:13).

In 1 Corinthians 3, as we will see in some detail, Paul talks about *you* and *me* being a *building* – what we today would call the superstructure over a foundation (verse 9). We – God's people – are his 'building' and are thus temples of the Holy Spirit (1 Cor. 3:16). And that is what Hebrews 3:6 means, quoted at the beginning of this chapter: 'we are his house' – God's house, dwelling place, building or superstructure.

It is a both sobering and thrilling honour to be called God's 'house', for that is what you and I are. God has put us on our honour to build that house, or superstructure, in accordance with our Architect's glorious blueprint. As the tabernacle in the wilderness was to be a copy of the real one in heaven (Exod. 25:40), so are you and I intended to be God's 'house' – as he has willed for us in heaven.

In 1 Corinthians 3 Paul tells us what the ingredients, or materials, of this house are to be. We are presented with two possibilities, two sets of materials: either (1) gold, silver or precious stones, or (2) wood, hay and straw (verse 12).

Paul states it in much the same way to Timothy: 'In a large house there are articles not only of gold and silver, but also of wood and clay; some are for noble purposes and some for ignoble' (2 Tim. 2:20). This means that the same house can be a mixture of the good, the bad and the ugly. Our mandate is to be cleansed from what is ignoble in order that we may be instruments for 'noble purposes, made holy, useful to the Master and prepared to do any good work' (2 Tim. 2:21). When we have been cleansed in this manner, we will therefore build God's house wisely – with the materials that bring him honour and glory. But if we are not so cleansed, we will foolishly erect a superstructure of materials that will be burned up on the Day of days. And, as I said, God may expose us in advance of that Day.

Wisdom and sexual purity

When I say it is no 'accident' that a person is found out, I need to make two observations: (1) In his own sovereign time and manner, God decides to roll up his sleeves and judge – as he did with King David (2 Sam. 12). God simply stepped in and did what he felt he had to do. (2) It is not an accident, but predictable, when a person falls grievously. It didn't just 'happen', although it may appear that way. For a grievous fall is the consequence of a failure to prepare adequately for the test – to which I will return below.

Let me address you if you are one who has not only fallen, but somehow got caught and been exposed. I risk saying things that can make you feel guilty – which, believe me, is the last thing I want to do as you already have enough guilt on your plate and I have no desire to add to that. The problem is, when I point out the ingredients that make for a superstructure with gold, silver and gems, you may get the feeling that you are reading this 'too late'. So why should you read this?

My answer is: because there is hope; there is time; it is not too late. For any teachable person who has fallen, God would not put this book in your hands to condemn you or leave you without hope. You can begin *now* to rebuild your superstructure. I will have a lot more to say on this when, below, we take a look at the life of David. In the meantime, if your attitude is one of wanting to get it right from this point, all I write, I can assure you, is aimed to help you – not to make you feel 'if only I had done that'.

In other words, if you don't 'dig in your heels' as some have done when they were exposed, God can use you again. My loving suggestion is this: welcome the disciplining of the Lord as you would an honoured guest. If you do this, you will heal inwardly and outwardly and God can make things happen for you and use you again. 'Though you have made me see troubles, many and bitter, you will restore my life again; from the depths of the earth you will again bring me up. You will increase my honour and comfort me once again' (Ps. 71:20–21).

But if you resent the fact that you got caught, and point the finger at whoever it was who 'blew the whistle' on you and refuse to accept the counsel of those in authority over you, you will never, never, never come back.

When I think of certain leaders (some of them being my friends) who got exposed in recent years, and I observe their reaction – refusing to accept wise advice and loving discipline – my heart aches. I often think of those who could be back in the place of strategic ministry today, but who will remain yesterday's men, yesterday's women. Why? Because they refused to accept the discipline that was required by those who were willing to help them. For some, then, I fear it is too late.

But not you, and that is why I have written this book. So bear with me in what I say. Not a single word is designed to give you a heavy, guilty feeling, but only a light sense of God's beckoning to put things right.

Our whole lives can be called *preparation for a test*. Like it or not, we are – day and night – always erecting a superstructure. That is why we are called 'God's house'. It is our daily choice of materials for the house that we are building that matters. If, for example, you and I choose wood, hay, straw or clay when building the superstructure, it is setting ourselves up for an inevitable crash; our fall is predictable. If, on the other hand, we choose to erect a superstructure with gold, silver and gems, we will not be likely to fall here on earth, nor be ashamed at the Judgement Seat of Christ. I will explain later how these metaphors are to be applied.

It may surprise you how closely wisdom and understanding are connected to sexual purity. You see it again and again in the book of Proverbs. Early on in this amazing book of Scripture we learn that 'the fear of the Lord is the beginning of knowledge, but fools despise wisdom and discipline' (Prov. 1:7). Wisdom is what saves one 'from the adulteress, from the wayward wife with her seductive words' (Prov. 2:16). 'How long will you simple ones love your simple ways? How long will mockers delight in mockery and fools hate knowledge? If you had responded to my rebuke, I would have poured out my heart to you and made my thoughts known to you. But since you rejected me when I called and no-one gave heed when I stretched out my hand, since you ignored all my advice and would not accept my rebuke, I in turn will laugh at your disaster; I will mock when calamity overtakes you – when calamity overtakes you like a storm, when disaster sweeps over you like a whirlwind, and when distress and trouble overwhelm you' (Prov. 1:22–27). (See also Prov. 5:1–14, 20–23, 7:1–27.) It can all be summed up in this verse: 'A man who commits adultery lacks judgment; whoever does so destroys himself' (Prov. 6:32). Consider how these proverbs repeat themselves: 'Say to wisdom, "You are my sister," and call understanding your kinsman; they will keep you from the adulteress, from the wayward wife with her seductive words' (Prov. 7:4–5). These verses should be applied in exactly the same way when homosexual practice is involved.

What I have quoted in the previous paragraph can be summed up as this: if a person has rejected the fear of the Lord – which is the beginning of wisdom and understanding – his or her fall as a result of sexual temptation cannot be a surprise. It would have been only a matter of time. Furthermore, falling into sexual sin is not only foolish; it causes one to forfeit the promise of a greater understanding. Speaking personally, I *live* for understanding, wisdom and insight. One of my greatest fears is that I might accept doctrinal error. Falling into sexual sin removes my hope that God will give me insight from his Word.

To put it another way: choosing the correct materials for building God's house is a way of preventing sexual sin. Rejecting the ingredients that erect a faulty superstructure (wood, clay, hay and straw) is what Paul means by being *cleansed* from dishonourable motives so that we are instruments of 'noble purposes, made holy, useful to the Master and prepared to do any good work' (2 Tim. 2:21).

However, building God's house with clay or straw does not refer only to sexual matters; we will see that the superstructure covers the whole of our lives – our bodies, souls and spirits. But because so much, sadly, that pertains to a grievous fall relates to a moral or sexual failure, we must give due attention to this area.

We – you and I – are God's house. 'Unless the Lord builds the house, its builders labour in vain' (Ps. 127:1). This amazing verse mainly refers to our embarking on a project that God is *not* in – to show the folly of trying to build what is not his idea. In a word: it won't work! But when it comes to our building the superstructure, you can be sure that God is behind our selecting the right materials. He does not want a superstructure that will not stand the test. So remember: in building God's house, this is something he is *in* – and you have him behind you all the way.

2

Ending Well

Well done, good and faithful servant! You have been faithful with a few things; I will put you in charge of many things. Come and share your master's happiness! (Matt. 25:23)

Therefore, my brothers, be all the more eager to make your calling and election sure. For if you do these things, you will never fall, and you will receive a rich welcome into the eternal kingdom of our Lord and Saviour Jesus Christ. (2 Pet. 1:10–11)

For I am already being poured out like a drink offering, and the time has come for my departure. I have fought the good fight, I have finished the race, I have kept the faith. Now there is in store for me the crown of righteousness, which the Lord, the righteous

Judge, will award to me on that day – and not
only to me, but also to all who have longed for
his appearing. (2 Tim. 4:6–8)

Best of all, God is with us.

The last words of John Wesley (1703–91)

The older I get, the faster times flies; the older I get, the
more I cry out to God, 'Let me end well.'

I have been amazed at the number of people, and in
particular church leaders, who did not end well – because
of either a moral failure or a spiritual deficiency. Sometimes a sad death bed state comes from a lack of assurance
concerning salvation – as in the case of the great Puritan
preacher William Perkins (1558–1602). Strange as it may
seem, and godly though he was, Perkins spent much of his
preaching life stressing assurance of salvation, but he died
without it himself. A large part of my Oxford thesis
centred on Perkins's emphasis of 2 Peter 1:10 ('make your
calling and election sure').

William Perkins taught that assurance of salvation was
to be based on godly living, but he actually died not
knowing for sure if he himself was truly saved. I would
hate to die like that. It was not that he became less than
godly in the end. No, it was because he was a victim of his
own theology: he put the ground of assurance at such a
high level that to know that you were saved was out of
reach for most people. He insisted that assurance of

salvation came through the maintenance of sanctification, or good works. Such sanctification was to be based upon carefully keeping the Ten Commandments and the Sermon on the Mount. This observance must be exhibited day and night in thought, word and deed. The basis of assurance of salvation became beyond the grasp not only of so many of his followers, but even of Perkins himself.

When I first came to Westminster Chapel, I was continually surprised by the number of good people who would come into the vestry after a sermon and say that my own preaching gave them hope that they were truly converted after all! 'What?' I would say to them. 'Here you are, a professing Christian for all these years, and you have not been sure whether you will go to heaven when you die?' Sadly, that was all too often the case. It was not a matter of moral scandal in their private lives, but a theology that put assurance out of reach for conscientious people. Many of these folk were avid readers of the Puritans. Some of them were theologically acute, but spiritually deprived.

But far worse than this would be coming to the end of one's life and being remembered almost entirely for a moral failure, a lack of integrity or having been involved in a financial scandal. It is like Watergate with Richard Nixon, or the moral failure of Bill Clinton. They will not be largely remembered for good things they no doubt did when in the White House. In any case, so many brilliant lives – in the secular world and in the Church – have ended under a cloud. What is more, such people come from every conceivable theological and church background. I am talking about Evangelicals, Fundamentalists, Reformed, Baptists, Presbyterians, Nazarenes, Methodists, Episcopalians, Anglicans, Catholics, Pentecostals and Charismatics. There is *no* theology that can guarantee transparent character if the person does not want to honour God in his or her life both day and night. It has happened to the best of men and women, and could happen to any of us. As for those of us still living, though, it is not too late to end well.

The man I was named after, Dr R. T. Williams, would exhort, when ordaining people to the ministry: 'Young men, beware of two things: money and women; because if your ministry is characterized by a scandal regarding either of these, God will forgive you but the people won't.'

The Apostle Paul ended well. He said so in what was almost certainly his last epistle, when he wrote to Timothy: '. . . I have finished the race, I have kept the faith. Now there is in store for me the crown of righteousness, which the Lord, the righteous Judge, will *award* to me on that day' (2 Tim. 4:7–8). Paul did not have such confidence early on; he said to the Corinthians, 'I beat my body and make it my slave so that after I have preached to others, I myself will not be disqualified for the prize' (1 Cor. 9:27). This was written around AD 50. But some fifteen years later he could say to Timothy, just before he was beheaded in Rome, that he would receive the crown he aspired to. He was not worried about whether he was saved when he wrote those words in 1 Corinthians 9:27; he was very concerned that he not be rejected for the prize – a reward that is on offer in addition to salvation.

As we will see, rewards will be handed out at the Judgement Seat of Christ. I have heard people say, 'I don't care about getting a reward after I die, I just want to make it to heaven.' I don't mean to be unfair, but I have never thought a comment like this reflected a very deep spirituality. It sometimes even smacks of false modesty, as in the old song I heard as I grew up, 'Lord, build me just a cabin in the corner of glory land' – as if one did not want a spectacular mansion, only a cabin! The truth is, although I don't know precisely what a reward in heaven entails (other than God saying 'Well done'), I know it was of deep concern to Paul, who wanted it almost more than anything – and who could say in the end that he *got* it.

This brings the importance of the Judgement Seat of Christ before us. It cannot be stated too firmly or too often that one of the main reasons we have this very teaching in the New Testament is not only to show that God will have the Final Word but that, knowing we will stand before the Lord Jesus Christ on the Last Day, the anticipation of this event might change our lives in the here and now. That is why Paul added, 'Knowing therefore the terror of the Lord, we persuade men' (2 Cor. 5:11 – AV). He included himself, as well as you and me, when he stated that '*we* must *all* appear before the judgment seat of Christ, that each one [of us] may receive what is due to him for the things done while in the body, whether good or bad' (2 Cor. 5:10). This is not a reference to the judgement of the lost, who go to hell, but what happens to the saved.

In a word, saved people will have to give an account of the things done *while in the body*. The reward will therefore be based on how you lived on earth.

I find it so interesting that the same Apostle Paul who spent much of his life stressing justification by faith alone and salvation by sheer grace also had the most to say about a 'reward' at the Judgement Seat of Christ! That is why Paul said, 'I beat *my body* and make it my slave.' Why? Not because he thought he had to do that to make it to heaven. After all, salvation is by grace, not works (Eph. 2:8–9). Paul's fear was not missing out on heaven, but being rejected for the 'prize'. In other words, he was not talking about whether he would or would not get to heaven; he was speaking about something *in addition* to going to heaven – or, you could say, *in advance* of getting to heaven: a reward at the Judgement Seat of Christ on the Last Day.

We should know therefore that Paul was not the slightest bit worried about being rejected for entry into heaven. It was the *prize* he was worried about. The word 'prize' (Greek: *brabion* – used also in Phil. 3:14) is used inter-changeably with 'crown' (Greek: *stephanos* – used eighteen times in the New Testament) and 'reward' (Greek: *misthos* – used twenty-nine times), and often with 'inheritance' as well (Greek: *kleronomia* – used at least seventeen times to mean 'reward', as in Col. 3:24).

One of the clearest but most neglected teachings in the

New Testament is the distinction between salvation and *reward*. All who rest on the foundation, namely, Jesus Christ (1 Cor. 3:11), will be saved. They are assured of heaven. That is *given* to us – it is a free gift (Rom. 6:23). But not all who are saved will receive a *reward* (1 Cor. 3:14–15), which we will see in more detail below.

It was the *reward*, then, that Paul was after. He could not bear the thought of seeing others get a reward, but finding himself being rejected for this reward, crown or prize. But he knew that this was possible, and he dreaded the shame of being openly rejected for this prize more than anything. That is why he kept his 'body' under subjection (1 Cor. 9:27).

What the Authorised Version translates as 'castaway' in 1 Corinthians 9:27, and is translated 'disqualified for the prize' in the New International Version, comes from the Greek *adokimos* – which means 'rejected'. The fuller meaning of *adokimos* means 'tested, but not approved'. The Hebrew equivalent is used in Jeremiah 6:30: 'They are called rejected silver, because the Lord has rejected them.' All of us will be tested on that Day – by fire. But not all of the saved will be approved. This is because some saved people did not end well; their works will be burned up.

Paul knew this could happen to him. I know it could happen to me. Do you realise it could happen to you?

Speaking personally, I don't know of any doctrine in Scripture that has had greater impact on me than this.

Frankly, I myself am not worried about being eternally lost, but I *do* worry about being rejected for the 'prize' at the Judgement Seat of Christ – the very thing that Paul was concerned about. This motivates me to live a transparent, pure and godly life more than I can possibly describe. It is before me all the time. It pulls me forward, it keeps me on my knees, and mercifully has kept me from succumbing to temptation when I might have given in. What is more, like Paul, I know that my converts and those who have listened to me and read my books will *see for themselves* whether I am genuine or phoney on that Day.

Some of my fears

Let me share some of my deep fears with you. I am not talking about a 'spirit of fear' (2 Tim. 1:7) – that is, a dread, timidity or terror engendered by the devil. No, I am talking about honest concerns that trouble me when I think about ending well.

My first concern is that *God might take his hand off me – and leave me alone*. I am reminded of those ominous words, 'Ephraim is joined to idols; leave him alone!' (Hos. 4:17). I cannot think of anything worse than for God to leave me alone. It is said of those who rejected the knowledge of creation clearly revealed to the conscience, that God merely 'gave them over' (Rom. 1:24, 26). As my old friend Rolfe Barnard used to say, 'Paul didn't say that

God "clubbed" them or "pushed" them; he just *gave them up.*'

The psalmist dreaded God's 'hot displeasure' (Ps. 38:1 – AV), but C. H. Spurgeon implied that there was something worse than that – God's cold shoulder: 'who can stand before his cold?' (Ps. 147:17 – AV). This is when God *ceases to deal with a person*, and it is precisely what Hebrews 6:4–6 means by a person who cannot be renewed again to repentance.

Billy Graham said some time ago that his worst fear was that God would take his hand off him. It is my fear too. It can't get worse than that. But it is exactly what happened to King Saul, as I said earlier. Let me remind you: here was a man who was chosen of God (1 Sam. 9:15–16), who had a brilliant beginning (1 Sam. 10:9–10), who lost the anointing of God's approval (1 Sam. 16:1, 18:12), and yet whose prophetic gift flourished simultaneously with his shameful behaviour (1 Sam. 19:18–24). This was Saul on his way to kill young David, because David was such a threat; and yet Saul prophesied as if he still had God's total favour.

In other words, King Saul's gift flourished as if all was well and as though his relationship with God was as it once had been; as if nothing bad had happened in the meantime.

It reminds me of that terrifying statement by the episcopal rector some years ago who said that if the Holy Spirit were taken completely from the Church today, 90 per cent of the work of the Church would carry on *as if nothing had happened*. That can happen to any church, and it can happen to an individual. It is what happened to Saul, and it is what could happen to you and me. This is the kind of theology that the Apostle Paul was immersed in. It explains his fear of being 'disqualified for the prize' in 1 Corinthians 9:27. The Hebrew equivalent of the Greek word we looked at above – *adokimos* – is used of King Saul: 'I have rejected him as king' (1 Sam. 16:1). But Saul continued on as if nothing had happened.

It is so easy for either a God-given natural ability or a gift of the Holy Spirit, as in 1 Corinthians 12: 7–11, to camouflage our true, secret relationship with God.

My second fear is that *I might teach what is not exactly true*. I cannot bear the thought that I would pass on any measure of theological error. I suppose some people do not worry too much about whether they hold to sound theology. But I do. It is my life. I want to get it right in my thinking before I stand in a pulpit or take a pen in my hand. One day I will have to give an account of every sentence I have written, every word I have uttered (in and out of the pulpit), including every 'careless' word (Matt. 12:36).

What is my assurance that I will not accept or teach heresy? I answer: one thing – my obedience to the Holy Spirit. My guarantee of sound theology is not my training, my mentors, my reading or my level of intelligence; it is unconditional obedience to the will of God. I put all my eggs into this basket – Jesus' words: 'If any man will do his will, he shall know of the doctrine, whether it be of God, or whether I speak of myself' (John 7:17 – AV). I do not say that this verse promises to deliver a perfect theology to all who aspire to do God's will – whether or not they are trained or well read. But I do think it promises to keep us from any *serious* theological error when our relationship with God is right.

Here is why. If I have not grieved the Holy Spirit through bitterness (or whatever else grieves him – see Ephesians 4:30–5:7), I can expect to have the full benefit of the promise from Jesus that the Holy Spirit will guide me into 'all truth' (John 16:13). When I grieve the Spirit, the anointing temporarily lifts and I cannot think so clearly during this time or enjoy the benefits of the promises that pertain to the Holy Spirit, as given in chapters 14, 15 and 16 of John's Gospel. But when I am granted repentance and am changed from glory to glory (2 Cor. 3:18), I am given insights that are good, solid and true. To be honest, it is what I live for. Nothing – absolutely nothing – thrills me more than a fresh insight that comes from the immediate and direct work of the Holy Spirit. I therefore fear that I might somehow *imagine* I have an insight from the Holy Spirit, when in fact it is of the flesh. No theologian, however godly, learned or honest, is infallible.

Third, I fear that *I could be out of the will of God and not know it*. If this could happen to Joseph and Mary, it could happen to you or me. They went an entire day without Jesus, but assumed the whole time 'he was in their company' (Luke 2:44). I based my book *The Sensitivity of the Spirit* (Hodder) largely on this account. It is so easy to take the will and presence of God for granted.

I am sobered when I recall that God is no respecter of persons, that he will not bend the rules for any of us. If he didn't bend the rules for Joseph and Mary, he won't do it for you or me! If we proceed without him, we too are *on our own*.

The only prevention I know of is to develop an intimate knowledge of the *ways* of the Holy Spirit. The more familiar I am with his Presence and his ways, the more likely it is that I will *instantly sense his absence* when I move ahead without him.

To be fair, I don't think anyone of real faith can get seriously out of God's will for very long without his or her heart longing for his Presence. But I do not want to go a day, not even an hour, knowingly, without his conscious Presence.

Fourth, I fear that *I might discover that I could have had much more of God and been used in a greater manner but for my stubbornness to recognise his warnings*. I have made so many mistakes over the past fifty years, and I would give anything to have a second chance in certain areas (especially with my family). I know I am a forgiven man, though. I have forgiven myself – totally – as I explained in my book *Totally Forgiving Ourselves* (Hodder). Furthermore, I put my trust in Romans 8:28: 'And we know that all things work together for good to them that love God, to them who are the called according to his purpose' (AV). I believe in that promise with all my heart.

But I admit at the same time that I sometimes wonder how much better it might have been had I listened to clear cautions from the Lord over the years. This is why I am so keen not to brush aside any loving word from a friend or stranger – lest I miss all that God would do with me. The older you get, the more you want to avoid any past mistakes.

Fifth, I fear that *I might not hear God say to me, 'Well done'*. You may say that all Christians get that very same commendation when they get to heaven, but I don't agree. A 'rich welcome' is promised on certain conditions (2 Pet. 1:11). This is one of several reasons I believe that not everyone who goes to heaven will get the same reward, or even that everyone will get *some* reward. As we will see below, only those who have built a superstructure made of gold, silver and costly stones will receive a reward. Those who built a house made of wood, hay or straw will have their whole superstructure 'burned up'; they will 'suffer loss' (of reward), but none the less 'will be saved, but only as one escaping through the flames' (1 Cor. 3:14–15).

As for those people who say, 'I don't care about a reward, I just want to make it to heaven', I know what they mean by that. After all, the difference between heaven and hell is infinite and incalculable. Those who are spared eternal punishment and make it to heaven have a debt to God that can never be paid. It was paid by the blood of Jesus and we can never take any credit for it. But God wants all of his children not only to have an eternal home in heaven, but to be awarded the *crown*. It is therefore pleasing to God that we show gratitude *now* by living disciplined, God-honouring lives that will be rewarded. Yes, *rewarded*. Paul could say just before the end that the Lord would 'award' him 'the crown of righteousness' (2 Tim. 4:8).

The hymn writer Charles Wesley (1707–88) was moved by Revelation 4:10, when the twenty-four elders 'lay their crowns before the throne'. Wesley must have been on tiptoes of divine inspiration when he penned the lines:

> *Changed from glory into glory, till in heaven we take*
> *our place,*
> *Till we cast our crowns before Thee, lost in wonder,*
> *love and grace.*

So, to those of you who say, 'I don't care about a crown or prize or reward, I just want to make it to heaven', I ask: 'How do you think you will feel on that Day when you have no crown to cast before the throne? When those around you have the inestimable privilege of taking off the crowns from their heads and then laying them before King Jesus?' I should think it would be a most horrible, embarrassing and even shameful feeling to be seen without a crown.

I want to end well and, like you, I want to live a long time. In fact, we *all* want to end well. In an age when there seem to be more and more shocking revelations of those we esteemed so highly (I keep asking, 'Who will be next?'), I urge you to fall on your knees and cry out, 'O Lord, let it not be me'. To make sure you are not one of those who are exposed, it will mean following Paul's example: 'I beat my body and make it my slave so that after I have preached to others, I myself will not be disqualified for the prize' (1 Cor. 9:27).

Remember: one of the reasons we have the New Testament teaching about rewards at the Judgement Seat of Christ is that it will change our lives.

If you, then, are a fallen servant of Christ, but take these words with meekness and a teachable spirit, following the blueprint for a solid superstructure will enable you to be restored. 'You will increase my honour and comfort me once again' (Ps. 71:21).

3

God's Blueprint

By the grace God has given me, I laid a
foundation as an expert builder, and someone
else is building on it. But each one should be
careful how he builds. For no-one can lay any
foundation other than the one already laid,
which is Jesus Christ. If any man builds on this
foundation using gold, silver, costly stones,
wood, hay or straw, his work will be shown.

(1 Cor. 3:10–13)

My hope is built on nothing less than Jesus'
blood and righteousness; I dare not trust the
sweetest frame, but wholly lean on Jesus' Name.
On Christ the solid Rock, I stand; all other
ground is sinking sand.

Edward Mote (1797–1874)

Before we proceed, I must ask you a fundamental question: are you sure you are saved? I hope you won't feel insulted by my asking this – assuming you are a seasoned believer. But the easiest thing in the world is to take for granted what is most important – namely, whether someone knows for certain that, if they died today, they would go to heaven.

At Westminster Chapel I introduced Evangelism Explosion (EE), founded by Dr D. James Kennedy. It is the best soul-winning programme I know of. I will never forget how a very mature person, a doctor, took EE in London in order to learn how to lead *others* to Christ, then realised during this course that she herself had not been truly converted! In other words, she was saved as a result of learning EE.

It is possible that some people who have fallen were not even converted. If you are truly converted, then you won't mind reading this chapter. If it should turn out that you have *not* been saved, it is absolutely crucial that you read every sentence in this chapter. There can hardly be anything worse than building a superstructure on a faulty foundation.

The foundation

I must ask you: do *you* know for sure that, if you were to die today, you would go to heaven? If you do not know for sure, read on. If the answer is yes, then I must ask you another question: if you were to stand before God (and you will) and he were to ask you (which he might do), 'Why should I let you into heaven?', what exactly would you say?

Be honest. Imagine it. You are standing before God and you must state why you truly believe you should be granted entrance into heaven. What would you say to God? Here are typical answers (I have asked this of thousands of people over the years): 'I have tried to live a good life'; 'I have done my best'; 'I believe in God'; 'I have been baptised'; 'I was brought up in a Christian home – and have been a Christian all my life'; 'I have been sanctified'; 'I go to Holy Communion'; 'I went forward and prayed in a service'; 'I bowed at an altar of prayer'; 'I prayed through'; 'I live by the Golden Rule'; 'I have kept the Ten Commandments'; 'I live by the Sermon on the Mount'; 'I pray to God every day'; 'I have tried to be a good Christian example'; 'I love God'; 'I have tried to be godly'; 'I go to church regularly'.

I would have to say that if any of the above answers would be what you would say to God, believing that is what qualifies you for getting inside the Pearly Gates, I have to tell you (with respect): you are probably not a converted person.

There is basically only *one* answer that shows you are resting solidly on the true foundation: that your reliance for salvation is on Jesus Christ alone – his blood and righteousness. If you know in your heart of hearts that

34

your only hope of getting into heaven is because Jesus Christ *paid your debt on the cross*, you are in good shape! This is because the blood of Jesus shed on the cross cried out for justice – and got it! Jesus Christ who is the God-man *satisfied God's justice* on your behalf by his shed blood on the cross. Never forget that Jesus was and is God. He was and is God as though he were not man, and yet man as though he were not God. He is fully God, fully man. When *you transfer the trust* you had in your good works *to* what Jesus the God-man did for you on the cross, God declares you righteous in his sight (Rom. 4:5). God declares you *saved*. That is the foundation – the only secure foundation. 'For no-one can lay any foundation other than the one already laid, which is Jesus Christ' (1 Cor. 3:11).

> *My hope is built on nothing less than Jesus' blood and righteousness; I dare not trust the sweetest frame, but wholly lean on Jesus' Name.*
> Edward Mote (1797–1874)

Are you on that foundation? That is the first question that must be asked. Do you know you are saved? If so, you are qualified to build a superstructure – God's house – on top of that foundation.

One of Paul's favourite phrases to denote that we are on this foundation is 'in Christ'. He puts these words – 'in Christ' – together many times. Take a look at how often these two words come together in Paul's epistles – dozens of times. This is because those who have transferred their trust *from* their good works *to* what Jesus did for them (putting all their eggs into one basket) are said to be 'in Christ'.

Perhaps I have not told you anything you did not already know backwards and forwards. But do you ever pause to focus on the fact that being *in Christ* implies so much?

Even the non-Christian often has a fairly shrewd idea of what the Christian is supposed to be like. But do you sometimes find yourself embarrassingly *unlike* what you should be? I have to admit that I do. For example, 'If anyone is in Christ, he is a new creation; the old has gone, the new has come!' (2 Cor. 5:17). The old has *gone*? What am I to believe when the 'old' seems to return? Furthermore, 'God raised us up with Christ and seated us with him in the heavenly realms in Christ Jesus' (Eph. 2:6). That being true, how can earthly things possibly matter to me again? I'm sorry, but they sometimes do! Not only that, but 'he who began a good work in you will carry it on to completion until the day of Christ Jesus' (Phil. 1:6) suggests an inevitably good outcome. And yet some fall after their conversion.

The very same promises quoted above would have been applied to the man in Corinth whose sin was incest (1 Cor. 5:1–5); to Ananias and his wife, Sapphira, who were instantly struck down dead for lying to the Holy Spirit (Acts 5:1–10); to Demas, who 'loved this world' (2 Tim. 4:10), and to Alexander the metalworker, who did Paul great harm (2 Tim. 4:14).

What went wrong? Some people dismiss all the examples in the previous paragraph by saying that 'they were never converted in the first place'. Really? How can they be so sure? How often some of us love to protect our doctrinal biases! Would we have said this – that his real problem was that he was not a true believer – about King David immediately after he committed adultery and then ordered Uriah's execution? Or about Simon Peter at the time he denied knowing the Lord? It is a fact that, sadly, truly saved people can, and sometimes do, fall.

Not all who make a profession of faith are saved, as the Parable of the Sower makes clear (Matt. 13:3–23). But the writers of Scripture lead us to assume that the people I mentioned above believed the gospel as much as anybody else who is said to believe. I also know that 'the best of men are men at best' and therefore that the *best* of God's servants – men or women – can fall.

I also know that God can take the fallen and restore them.

The superstructure

When Paul said, '. . . you are God's field, God's building' (1 Cor. 3:9), he used two metaphors – one referring to natural vegetation, the other to that of erecting a material structure. He had just said, 'I planted the seed, Apollos watered it, but God made it grow' (1 Cor. 3:6). That is why he said we are 'God's field' or 'garden' (Living Bible). Paul might have stayed with that metaphor and even given us an exposition of John 15:1–17 – Jesus' discussion of the vine and the branches. For what Jesus taught about the vine and branches is very like what Paul says about a building in 1 Corinthians 3:9–15.

When Paul switched the metaphor from a garden to that of a building he used the word *oikodome*, which in this place means two things simultaneously: (1) the *act* of building, and (2) the superstructure – what is *above* a foundation. The act of building is what God does through us – not what he does by himself without us, or what we do without him. 'In this work, we work with God' in order to erect the house he has planned (1 Cor. 3:9 – Phillips Modern English). God's 'building' therefore refers both to the act of building and to our erecting the superstructure he has in mind for us.

This is what we are – his building, the result of his grace in our lives.

The writer of the epistle to the Hebrews takes the same line: 'And we are his house [*oikos* – a word in the same family as in 1 Cor. 3:9], if we hold on to our courage and the hope of which we boast' (Heb. 3:6). In other words, you and I are God's property – his house, his dwelling-place, his superstructure, *even his temple*, as Paul will go on to say in 1 Corinthians 3:16–17.

One might therefore hastily assume that if God does the building, we need not worry – he will do it all! After all, if

God builds anything it is inevitably going to be flawless and magnificent. But that is not necessarily the case. Even with vegetation there was the co-operative effort between Paul's planting and Apollos' watering; but it was God who made it grow, or 'gave the increase' (AV).

You may have heard the story about the meticulous gardener who managed to cultivate and grow the most beautiful garden in the area. Someone said to him, 'The Lord has certainly given you a lovely garden.' 'Right,' said the man, 'but you should have seen it when the Lord had it all to himself!'

This would be the same with God's building – the superstructure. It is therefore both what God does and what we do. Having stated that he laid the foundation, knowing that he had presented sound doctrine to his followers on a silver platter, Paul added these words: 'Each one should be careful how he builds' (1 Cor. 3:10).

Paul laid the foundation, but he could not build the superstructure for each of his hearers, or readers. It is up to us to build the superstructure over the foundation. So even though it is called God's building, it is none the less what you and I must do by erecting a superstructure upon the foundation. And lest someone misunderstand Paul and think he puts himself as the foundation, he makes sure that we understand: 'For no-one can lay any foundation other than the one already laid, which is Jesus Christ' (1 Cor. 3:11). In other words, the foundation is Jesus Christ. And those who trust Jesus, and the precious blood he shed on the cross, are converted and are *in Christ*. To quote again from the aforementioned hymn:

> *My hope is built on nothing less than Jesus' blood and righteousness; I dare not trust the sweetest frame, but wholly lean on Jesus' Name.*

All who can sing this hymn and mean every word of these lines in their heart of hearts are saved; this means they are on the foundation and qualified to build a superstructure. Those who cannot sing this and mean every word are still unconverted. This hymn is a good test of whether or not a person is truly a Christian. Many people may say the words, but in their hearts they are trusting anything but Jesus' blood – their good works, their baptism, their church membership, their gift, their knowledge of the Bible, or even their changed life.

The foundation, then, is Jesus Christ. I must repeat: you cannot build a superstructure unless you are on the foundation.

However, the house of God – which we are – is not perfect. It includes not only all who are saved, but also those who are saved and imperfect (which includes you and me). Indeed, 'In a large house there are articles not only of gold and silver, but also of wood and clay; some are for noble purposes and some for ignoble. If a man cleanses himself from the latter, he will be an instrument for noble purposes, made holy, useful to the Master and prepared to do any good work' (2 Tim. 2:20–21). That is a very important *if* – 'if a man cleanses himself . . .' That is precisely what you and I are required to do. That is what Paul means by being careful as to *how* we build on the foundation.

It is not a question of whether you and I are going to build a superstructure; it is a question of *what kind* of superstructure.

Character versus gift

Possibly the most important thing that can be said in this entire book is right here. It is that the quality of the superstructure *pertains to one's character, not one's gifts*. The gold, silver, precious stones, wood, hay or straw is not a reference to the brilliance of one's gift. A person may be an extraordinary orator, but this would not have anything to do with the quality of his or her superstructure. The ability to give a good speech or sermon has a natural explanation. Winston Churchill had a way with words, but this did not mean he was erecting a superstructure of gold, silver or precious gems when he was prime minister.

So too with the ability to make money, to practise law or medicine, to be a managing director or to preach well – it proves *nothing* with regard to erecting a solid superstructure. Or having the power to thrill an audience – whether by oratory or gifts of the Spirit. Or stirring a crowd so that they fall on their faces with the fear of the judgement of

God. The gift to do this is not what makes for a good superstructure. Even if I can preach on certain verses of the Bible with lucidity and simplicity, it is still not what will erect a solid superstructure; it is simply a gift I have regardless of my character. So also with an ability to prophesy, heal, cast out devils – or an ability to demonstrate stunning wisdom, as Ahithophel apparently had (2 Sam. 16:23). The gift of speaking in tongues likewise has nothing to do with building a superstructure.

This is the reason that both low-profile people and high-profile people can fall. They assume that if their *gift* is functioning under the power of the Spirit of God, they must be right with God. Wrong. For some people the matter of character does not seem to come into their heads. There are preachers who read the Bible not for intimacy with God, but only for sermons; if they preach well, they assume their relationship with Christ is good. Wrong again. There are people who have a gift of healing – and see people healed under their ministry. They believe that authentic healings validate their ministry and lifestyle. Wrong. There are prophetic people who assume that if they can call out people and tell them things about their personal lives that nobody but the person could know, this prophet must be an awesome man of God. Wrong yet again. We have seen that King Saul's prophetic gift functioned after the anointing of God's approval lifted from him (1 Sam. 18:10–12; 19:23).

You may ask: 'How can gifted preachers, high-powered

laymen, prophetic people and church leaders degenerate to such a level and operate with apparent success but without the approval of God?' I will try to answer that. They do so because they have managed to maintain a good income, to keep preaching, praying for people, prophesying, casting out demons – and live double lives without it affecting their ministry negatively (at first). Some such people, many of them well known, have carried on like this for years – and did not get caught. Some will get exposed, the rest will await God's wrathful judgement on the Final Day. I would not want to be in their shoes.

Many of them started well. There was a time when some of these people were totally dedicated to God and his glory – perhaps not all, but certainly some of them. I know what I am talking about because some of them told me this themselves. They not only dedicated themselves to God's glory, but made sacrifices to get where they got. They gave up homes and good jobs, resisted sexual temptation again and again, they did not care what people thought, they were prepared to look foolish to the world, they lived without incomes, barely survived by eating the cheapest sorts of food, were laughed at by the world – I could go on and on. These people started out in a manner that suggested their names could be added to Hebrews 11 – the chapter that describes what people did by faith. The world was not worthy of them.

But something happened. God began to bless them – with both followers, those who looked up to them, and often financial rewards too. There have been preachers and evangelists who suddenly found they no longer had to struggle as money flowed in. Before long they were staying in five-star hotels. More to the point, they began to *demand* five-star hotels. They were eating the best food that money can buy. Their anointing continued. But then temptations crept in – temptations regarding money as well as sexual temptation. They gave in a bit. They noticed that they still had power the next night at church. They began to covet a greater amount of money. They noticed they could still prophesy and cast out demons. They could preach with tremendous effectiveness. Their sinful behaviour increased. They could preach as well as ever; people responded as much as ever. Their gifts were intact as much as ever; the anointing they took for granted.

And then they fell. But almost nobody knew but God himself. That they were not exposed made them feel they were 'special' – as if they had indemnity, they were selected by God to do what others could not do. They lied to themselves and concluded that they had God's approval in this – that God knew they had special needs.

Some of this kind of behaviour is going on today. Others have got caught. Those who don't get caught begin to feel secure – they have managed to carry on for so long that they don't worry about being exposed.

What I am saying in these lines is, unfortunately, but the tip of the iceberg. This sort of thing is going on in both charismatic and evangelical circles, and sexual and financial scandals cross denominational and theological lines. I know more than I wish I knew about Christians who have lived double lives for years – and they seem to have got away with this.

Some Christians don't get caught because it is, sadly, pornography that has gripped them. Sex in secret. When church leaders attend conferences, hotel managers often report that the number of sex films ordered via room service goes up astronomically – an indication that the number-one sin among preachers is pornography.

But sometimes pornography does not satisfy and Christians become vulnerable to an actual affair – though they keep ministering to others the whole time. This is because, as I keep saying, the gifts and calling of God are irrevocable – without repentance. In other words, God does not bestow or withhold his gifts according to one's character – or spiritual life. They are sovereignly given, but God expects us to treat such gifts responsibly and with holy gratitude.

Jesus said that people would claim to do what they do in his very name! 'Lord, did we not prophesy in your name, and in your name drive out demons . . . ?' (Matt. 7:22). Hiding behind the name of Jesus gives some people a false sense of security; they assume 'all must be well' if they are doing what they do in the name of Jesus – as if God is going to give such people extraordinary protection.

He won't. He hates the sin more than the hurt he feels when his name is disgraced, and this is why he sends judgement on some – who are often his very best people, as in the case of King David. If God was prepared to expose the only man in the Bible called 'a man after his own heart', why should God not openly judge you or me?

The Lord building the house

One of my favourite Bible verses is: 'Unless the Lord builds the house, its builders labour in vain' (Ps. 127:1). This means that if God is not behind what you are trying to do – or build – it will fail, no matter how hard you try and how long you work at it.

But the Lord still does not build the house without builders. *He* builds it, yes, but he uses builders. Us!

Here is what you and I have going for us in building a brilliant and solid superstructure (as described in 1 Cor. 3): *God is behind what we are wanting to do* – if that means a desire to glorify God. In other words, we are not called to embark upon a project that is speculative or doubtful. A superstructure based on godly character and transparent honesty is inherent in God's blueprint for us. It is what God *wants* for you and me.

God's blueprint is designed to show what is best for us. For that reason we must take care *how* we build. The reason Christians fall is that they do not take care to build the kind of superstructure that follows his blueprint.

4

The Quality of the Superstructure

> If any man builds on this foundation using
> gold, silver, costly stones, wood, hay or straw,
> his work will be shown for what it is, because it
> will be revealed with fire, and the fire will test
> the quality of each man's work. If what he has
> built survives, he will receive his reward. If it is
> burned up, he will suffer loss; he himself will be
> saved, but only as one escaping through the
> flames. (1 Cor. 3: 12–15)

There is a broad distinction between character
and reputation, for one may be destroyed by
slander, while the other can never be harmed
save by its possessor. Reputation is in no man's
keeping. You and I cannot determine what other
men shall think and say about us. We can only

determine what they *ought* to think of us and
say about us. J. G. Holland (1819–81)

If I take care of my character, my reputation
will take care of itself.
D. L. Moody (1837–99)

In January of 1963 I had an unusual dream – of a boa
constrictor coming after me. In the dream this large
snake was a good distance away. I hoped it would not see
me, so I kept low and quiet as well as a fair distance away.
The next thing I knew it came straight for me and pounced
on me, and then I woke up.

A few days later some close friends in Fort Lauderdale,
where we were living, invited Louise and me to go to hear
a faith-healer/preacher in a large tent. So many of our
friends were mesmerised by this particular preacher,
saying, 'R. T., you *must* go and hear him.' So we did. On
the way into the tent I looked at some of the books he was
selling. One of them was based upon a denial of the deity
of Jesus Christ. That of course gave me pause for thought
even before the meeting had started.

We sat at the back, a good distance away from the pulpit.
But I already had a funny feeling that my dream of the big
snake was about to be fulfilled. The preacher left the
platform and called out people way up front. 'Have you
and I ever met before?' he would ask. 'No,' came the reply.
'Do you believe I am a man of God?' 'Yes,' would come the

reply. 'Do you believe God has told me something about you?' 'Yes,' they would say. And, sure enough, he would tell these people things that he could not have known. Everybody seemed to be thrilled.

I whispered to Louise, 'He will come up to me shortly.' 'Really?' she asked, 'Will he come all the way back here?' 'Yes, you will see.'

'Here he comes,' I said to Louise. He came to the back of the tent, passing up hundreds of people along the way, and came straight to me for some reason. He stood in front of me and asked me to stand. I did. 'Have you and I ever met before?' he asked. 'No,' I replied. 'Do you believe I am a man of God?' 'No,' I replied, as people gasped. 'Sir, have you and I ever met before?' 'No,' I said again. 'Do you believe God has told me something about you?' 'No,' I said, to everyone's astonishment. He asked a third time, 'Are you sure you and I have never met before?' I assured him we had not met. 'Do you believe God has told me something about you?' 'No,' I said again. Before I could reach for his microphone to explain why I was so adamantly against him, he took off like a scared rabbit, shouting to the crowd, 'Here is a man that is going straight to hell.'

My friends were upset with me. People hissed as we walked out of the tent. I felt a little bit odd, but knew I had been true to myself. I knew he was a phoney.

After we returned from London to the USA in 2002 I learned a few things about this man: that he was being sought by the police for financial fraud, that he had been refused by many Christian television stations, and that he was known by those around him for being openly homosexual. Not only that, though – he is now back on television, having found some stations that would take him.

It would be my own view that this man has never been converted. He is an unsaved man like those Jesus described, 'Did we not prophesy in your name, and in your name drive out demons and perform many miracles? Then I will tell them plainly, "I never knew you. Away from me, you evildoers!" ' (Matt. 7:22–23). Whereas I believe some high-profile people who have fallen *have* been truly converted years before, I do not think this particular man was ever saved. My reason for saying this is the kind of Christology he was upholding. A saved man would not propagate such ancient heresy (it was Arianism – the belief that Jesus was God's highest creation, but was not really God in the flesh).

This is one of the reasons I stressed the gospel and the right foundation in the previous chapter. People sometimes manage to get into the Church through the 'back door', as it were, like those described in 2 Peter 2:1–3 and Jude 4. This is why we must never take sound theology for granted.

And yet it is possible to be on the foundation – which means you are saved – and also to erect a superstructure made of wood, hay or straw, meaning you will have no reward at the Judgement Seat of Christ. These are materials that will be burned up on the Final Day. The person will be saved, according to Paul, but lose their reward (1 Cor. 3:15).

I turn again to you if you have fallen. If you know you are a saved person and that you will go to heaven when you die, the question before you now is: 'Will you rebuild a superstructure that will bring honour to God?' If you are a fallen man or woman, it is not too late to rebuild. This book has come to you in the gracious providence of God. He would not have given you hope if there were no hope.

The purpose of this chapter is twofold: (1) it will explain what is meant by Paul's metaphors: gold, silver, costly stones, wood, hay and straw; (2) to show you that your willingness to use the right materials from this point on in your life proves that God has mercifully granted repentance on your part and is evidence that you will be restored and used again.

If you have fallen it is almost certainly because you did not use the best ingredients to build God's house. I say this because one's fall is not 'accidental'; that is, it did not just 'happen' suddenly, but instead was the consequence of an ill-advised lifestyle. It is what Paul means by building a superstructure out of wood, hay and straw. The consequences of a faulty superstructure are revealed not only at the Judgement Seat of Christ; God may call one to give an account in this life – in advance of the Judgement.

Remember, we are *all* building a superstructure. Like it or not, it is not a question of *whether* you or I build a superstructure over the foundation; it is a matter of *what kind of ingredients* we use – whether gold, silver and precious stones, or wood, hay or straw. If you build your superstructure with gold, silver and precious stones, you will not fall. This is why Peter said, 'For if you do these things, you will never fall' (2 Pet. 1:10). By 'these things', Peter meant giving diligence to make your calling and election sure by adding to your faith, 'goodness; and to goodness, knowledge; and to knowledge, self-control; and to self-control, perseverance; and to perseverance, godliness; and to godliness, brotherly kindness; and to brotherly kindness, love' (2 Pet. 1:5–7).

But if you have fallen, you can rebuild – starting now if you have not begun already. If you are willing to do this, it shows a teachable spirit and beautiful evidence that you have a wonderful future. It shows too that you are unlike so many who resented (even rejected) any wisdom offered them after they fell and got caught.

Shortly after my friend Jack Taylor told me of our mutual friend's fall and exposure (see the beginning of Chapter 1), I wrote my friend an urgent letter. I pleaded with him, 'Don't be like —— [a well-known preacher whose fall was telecast around the world and became the butt of jokes by comedians].' It is widely known that the denomination of that fallen preacher required that he stay out of the ministry for two years. But no! He thundered back – deciding that three months of waiting was enough punishment! By refusing to accept his denomination's verdict to stay out of the ministry for that stipulated period of time, this famous preacher forfeited a restoration of his old anointing. I'm sorry to say it, but he will forever be yesterday's man as a result. So I pleaded with my friend, 'Please don't be like ——.' Sadly, though, he resented and rejected my counsel. That was only three years ago. If only he had listened. These three years have gone by so quickly. Many of his other friends warned him as well. Had he truly repented and submitted to those who were willing to help him, he would have been back in ministry today. Our God is a gracious, forgiving God. But my friend would not listen.

But if you are not like that, and instead are willing to build the kind of superstructure that Paul lays down in 1 Corinthians 3:12, you will not only be restored spiritually but – in God's time – be back in a place of usefulness again. What was true of David, Jonah and Simon Peter – all fallen, forgiven and restored men – will be true of you as well.

Understanding the metaphors of gold, silver and costly stones

I don't want to press the metaphors of gold, silver and costly stones too far. But I *do* know that there are basically three temptations all of us face every day, which come under the general heading of *money, sex and power*. I am sure there is more to it than that – namely, other things that might bring a person down (alcohol abuse, for example, or a lack of wisdom) – but I want to write about three main things (see the following chapter) that will build a God-honouring house: (1) integrity with money, (2) sexual purity, and (3) humility.

But first, why does Paul use gold, silver and costly stones as metaphors for building on the foundation?

Viability. This means things that are enduring. Something is viable according to its survival probability. Therefore Paul uses the metaphors of gold, silver and costly stones because they will survive fire. The point of a solid, lasting superstructure is whether it will survive the fire that will be revealed on the Final Day. Wood, hay and straw will obviously be burned up by the fire, but gold, silver and gems will not burn. 'The world and its desires pass away, but the man who does the will of God lives for ever' (1 John 2:17).

Virtue. Virtue means moral excellence. Gold, silver and costly stones indicate what is truly *good* as opposed to what is artificial, superficial or counterfeit. The super-structure you and I build must be based on transparent character. In a word: we must be *real*. I know what it is to ask the question of someone, 'Is he for real? Is she truly for real?' There are so many counterfeit people around nowadays that when you find someone is truly genuine it is a relief and feels like a breath of fresh air.

Visibility. Whereas the foundation is hidden, the super-structure is visible – a thing to be seen. Gold, silver and gems are tangible items that you can see. Furthermore, what is more beautiful than a glittering diamond or a genuine ruby or emerald? And what is more lovely than a true, open holy life? The Christian life is to be lived before the world:

> *T'was not the truth you taught, to you so clear, to me*
> * so dim;*
> *But when you came to me you brought a sense of*
> * Him.*
> *Yes, from your eyes He beckoned me, from your heart*
> * his love was shed*
> *When I lost sight of you and saw the Christ instead.*
>
> Anon.

Variety. Gold, silver and precious jewels indicate variety. So too with our superstructure. As Christians we are all differ-ent. My superstructure will not look like yours and yours will not look like mine. We all have different personalities, different backgrounds, different struggles, different weak-nesses, different strengths, different cultures and different faces!

Value. Probably the main reason Paul chooses gold, silver and gems is that they are valuable. There is certainly nothing cheap about them. Whereas wood, hay and straw are without value by comparison, God wants our lives to show true *worth*. There is nothing rarer than integrity, honesty, faithfulness and purity of life.

Therefore this question follows: how do we know that our own superstructure is comprised of gold, silver and precious stones, and not wood, hay or straw?

My answer is: by *application* of good teaching. Teaching must be applied, which means we must put it to practical use. It is not enough to hear and recognise good teaching; it is something we must make work in our lives. I remember going to east London years ago with some friends (who were great 'sermon tasters') to hear a great preacher who had come over from the USA. After the sermon they said, 'Wasn't that marvellous? Wasn't that wonderful?' But I feared immediately that they did not have the slightest intention of applying it to their own personal lives (as was later borne out).

We may get a good feeling when we hear profound teaching or great preaching. Or when singing a hymn. Or from reading the Bible. But that is not enough. We must *do* it as well as hear it. Otherwise we are like the person who 'looks at his face in a mirror and, after looking at himself, goes away and immediately forgets what he looks like' (James 1:23–24). It is like Paul's warning, '. . . you, then, who teach others, do you not teach yourself? You who preach against stealing, do you steal? You who say that people should not commit adultery, do you commit adultery?' (Rom. 2:21–22).

Take, for example, this very book. It is of no value if you do not apply this teaching. If you do not build a superstructure of gold, silver or gems, it would have been better had you not read this book.

But there is more. You build a good superstructure by how you treat temptation. Oscar Wilde said, 'I can resist anything but temptation.' When you give in to temptation you erect a superstructure of wood, hay or straw. When you resist it, you build a superstructure of gold, silver and costly stones. You may not *feel* that you are building anything. I don't think Joseph *felt* he was doing anything great when he resisted the flirtations of Potiphar's wife. He said 'no' to her and probably felt nothing. But the angels said 'yes!' because Joseph passed an important test in his life (see Gen. 39).

The colourful preacher Billy Sunday said that the reason Christians fall into sin so often is that they treat temptation like strawberry shortcake rather than like a rattlesnake! 'Clothe yourselves with the Lord Jesus Christ, and do not think about how to gratify the desires of the sinful nature' (Rom. 13:14). In other words, the best way to avoid falling into sin is to avoid the temptation. Most of us have a fairly shrewd idea of what – and who – will tempt us. If we willingly walk right into temptation, we are asking for trouble.

I know a man whose admitted weakness has been pornography. He has asked me to help him and I have prayed for him, and with him, about this. He has since in fact got the victory over pornography, but part of this victory came when he requested that a television set be removed from his room when he stayed in a hotel. He feared he would not have the strength to resist ordering a pornographic film, so he would ask that the television set be removed for as long as he was staying there. I don't think the hotel manager got many requests like that! But it was one way that my friend proved to himself (and to God) that he was deadly serious about getting the victory over pornography.

We build a superstructure that will survive fire by developing the right attitude towards any trial or testing. You cannot avoid trial. In this world you will have 'trouble' (John 16:33). But one thing we can do: develop an attitude that will *dignify the trial* when such testing comes.

God does not usually warn us that a trial is coming at such and such a time. If only he would say, when we are in a time of prayer and feeling his presence, 'Next Tuesday afternoon, R. T., you will notice the sudden withdrawal of my countenance, I will be hiding my face from you.' If only! No, it is not like that. It just *happens*. 'Truly you are a God who hides himself, O God and Saviour of Israel' (Isa. 45:15). No warning, no word from God – he just allows a time of testing to come without notice!

What are we to do? Expect it. Be prepared for it. Stay in an attitude of dignifying the trial rather than panicking and blaming God every time something negative happens. When you complain and grumble during the time of trial, the trial itself is actually doing you no good – plus the fact that you are, at best, building a house made of wood, hay and straw.

Dignifying the trial means: (1) not panicking when sudden testing comes, (2) no grumbling while it lasts, and (3) doing nothing to try to get it over with! Every trial has its own built-in time limit. All trials end. We may think they will last for ever, but they do end. And when the trial is over, the angels in heaven either blush or rejoice – based on whether or not you dignified the trial and helped to erect a superstructure of gold, silver and gems.

> *Every joy or trial cometh from above,*
> *Traced upon our dial by the sun of love;*
> *We may trust Him fully, all for us to do –*
> *They who trust Him wholly find him wholly true.*
>
> Frances Ridley Havergal (1836–79)

We build a permanent superstructure, one that will stand the test of fire, by controlling the tongue. You perhaps know that I have written a book called *Your Words Have Power* (Hodder). It is sobering to realise that you and I will 'have to give account on the day of judgement for every careless word' spoken (Matt. 12:36), which is probably my least favourite verse in the Bible!

We develop tongue control by not grumbling during a time of trial, but also by not telling anybody 'what they did to us' when you have been hurt by a person. Yes, you may need to pour your heart out for therapeutic reasons, but the main reason we tell 'what they did to us' is that we want to get vengeance – and punish those who have hurt us by making them look bad.

Every time you and I resist grumbling, gossiping, defending ourselves or making ourselves look good we build a superstructure that will survive the test of fire.

Understanding the metaphors of wood, hay and straw

The wood, hay and straw of 1 Corinthians 3:12 could refer to eccentric teaching as well as being a bad example of a Christian. For example, many Christians might hold to teaching that is less than biblical – through no fault of their own. It is possible that a sincere Christian could sit under teaching that is not based on sound theology. A person will be forgiven for that, but (happily) this teaching will be burned up at the Judgement Seat of Christ – and will not affect the person's salvation.

However, wood, hay and straw refer mainly to building a superstructure without the honour of God in mind. Sadly, there are those Christians who are saved because they are on a solid foundation, but their lives sometimes do not show their love for God. They consequently build a superstructure that will not stand the test of fire.

Why does Paul use these metaphors of wood, hay and straw?

They are corruptible. In other words, they are unable to be permanent. Wood, hay and straw are capable of decay, rot and becoming useless – unlike gold, silver and gems. It is not a good Christian who can be so easily lured away from the things of God and become so easily corrupted.

They are colourless. Unlike gold, silver and costly stones, wood, hay and straw are colourless and do not make a very attractive superstructure. As Christians we should have something about us that attracts the world, making them want what we have.

They are common. You can find wood, hay and straw without looking very hard, whereas precious metals and gems are uncommon. The Christian should radiate an aura that is exceedingly rare in the world. It is a sad day when we are so much like the world.

They are cheap. Wood, hay and straw are relatively worthless when compared to gold, silver and precious stones. The 'world was not worthy' of those people described in Hebrews 11 (verse 38) because they were anything but cheap and ordinary. Christians who are like this discredit the faith of Christ and his Name.

They are combustible. Wood, hay and straw are easily consumed when set on fire, but the superstructure we are invited to erect, that of gold, silver and costly gems, can never burn up.

The fiery trial

There are two kinds of trials that you and I can anticipate: (1) the fiery trials on earth – they are bound to come; we are 'destined' for them (1 Thess. 3:3). Peter said we should not be surprised by the fiery trial we are suffering (1 Pet. 4:16 – AV). But the ultimate test – the *trial of trials* – will be (2) the fiery trial above, when our superstructure will be shown for 'what it is, because the Day will bring it to light' by fire (1 Cor. 3:13).

What are the differences between the two trials? Both trials reveal exactly where we are spiritually. The trial here on earth tests our ability to manifest fruits of the Spirit. In the heat of the trial here in the world there will be an indication whether we are developing true Christian maturity – whether we panic, complain or dignify the trial. In other words, the heat of the trial on earth reveals the quality of our superstructure up to that point. It is a fairly good hint as to how we will come through at the Ultimate Trial – at the Judgement Seat of Christ.

The trial on the Final Day will be the very last test that will ever come to us; it is when the superstructure of wood, hay and straw will be burned up. After the trial on earth we can continue to repent and improve, having seen perhaps that we did not do too well. But there will be no chance to improve after the fiery trial above; it will be too late for further repentance.

The fiery trial below and the fiery trial above are alike in that both (1) are unexpected, coming without warning; (2) expose where we are in our spiritual progress; (3) will be a time of great pressure and testing; and (4) come from God.

These two trials are different in that (1) the trial on earth may be hidden from others, but the fiery trial on the Final Day will be out in the open – all will see where we are spiritually; (2) the trial below is brought on by earthly pressures – through people, persecution, financial troubles, ill health, etc., but the trial of the Judgement Seat of Christ will be God's fire without earthly pressures to show our spiritual state; (3) the trial below may come through a satanic attack; the trial above will come entirely by God's intervention of fire and great glory; and (4), as we saw earlier, whereas there is opportunity to put things right after a trial here below, it will be too late to improve or be granted repentance on the Day of days when the whole superstructure will be tested by God's fire.

The trial below *can* take its shape by God bringing judgement on us. This means being exposed – caught, found out. However painful this must be – and it will be very hard indeed, I can promise you – better now than then. However awful it must be to be judged in the here and now, it will be far, far worse then. This is partly why we have this word: 'Why should any *living* man complain when punished for his sins?' (Lam. 3:39). In other words, be thankful for it. It is far easier to receive God's fierce judgement now than on that Day. So Paul said, 'When we are judged by the Lord [whether through sickness or through premature death], we are being disciplined so that we will not be condemned with the world', which means we will not go to hell (1 Cor. 11:32). Hence at the Judgement Seat of Christ, if our superstructure is comprised of wood, hay and straw, at least we will be saved. Our works will be burned up, but we will be saved by fire (1 Cor. 3:15). But it will still be a terrible time for those who have no reward. I don't want that to be me.

Therefore the person whose superstructure is burned up will receive no reward. The reward comes to the one who built his house with gold, silver and precious stones. 'If what he has built survives, he will receive his reward' (1 Cor. 3:14).

If you have fallen and got exposed here on earth, God has been good to you. Don't complain to him. Thank him. One day you will be glad you did. Accept his judgement; it is so you will have another opportunity – not just for restoration and a rebuilding of God's house, but because God wants to use you again. What is more, this rebuilding of the superstructure not only means more time here on earth but also indicates that you could receive a great reward at the Judgement Seat of Christ.

Accept this teaching and you will be showing a genuine repentance already. Wait for him to show the next step forward. In the meantime, I would urge that you fall on your knees, thank God for his righteous judgements, and determine in your heart to rebuild your life along the lines of his blueprint. You cannot do better than that.

5

Money and Sex

But godliness with contentment is
great gain. (1 Tim. 6:6)

How then could I do such a wicked thing and
sin against God? (Gen. 39:9)

Young men, be careful about two things in your
ministry – money and women; for if there is a
scandal related to either of these, God will
forgive you, but the people won't.
R. T. Williams (1883–1946)

Most falls and failures in the Christian life can be traced
to impropriety with regard to one or more of these
three things: money, sex and power. I will devote the next
chapter to 'power'. As I said above, I am sure the list is
longer than that. A lack of wisdom, for example, can result

in one's fall. However, the fear of the Lord is the beginning of wisdom (Prov. 1:7), and when there is the proper fear of God in you, it follows that you will not lack any good thing (Ps. 34:10). 'He fulfils the desires of those who fear him; he hears their cry and saves them' (Ps. 145:19).

The fear of God will keep one from doing seriously stupid things – whether it be getting into trouble from a hot temper, feeding on gossip (which saps the spirit), caving in to bad advice, alcohol abuse, being undisciplined when it comes to food, abuse of prescription drugs, missing out on God's will for your life, or embracing serious theological error. In a word: the fear of God is the solution to avoiding these pitfalls.

But at the same time I think that you should make sure you have mastered three particular areas of your life – money, sex and power; this will require strong personal discipline and self-control. After all, one of the fruits of the Spirit is 'self-control' (Gal. 5:23). You will not only be erecting a superstructure of gold, silver and precious stones, but will almost certainly be kept from falling – which comes when you build a house in wood, hay and straw.

When Paul said that godliness with contentment is 'great gain' (1 Tim. 6:6), he might have put this remarkable state-ment in the context of sex, money or power. The context is about money, but the truth is that sex, money and power are so intertwined and related that it is sometimes difficult to discern which ingredient has the weightier influence on one's motivation. Regarding money, Paul wants us to be so content with the privilege of true godliness that eagerness for money is not an intense desire. Regarding sex, he wants us husbands to love our wives as Christ loved the Church (Eph. 5:25–33), so that the pursuit of godliness will remove adultery as a possibility. Regarding power, he wants us to love God and his approval so much that our sole ambition is to have his smile, not the admiration of our peers.

Integrity with money

I will quote yet again the warning of Dr R. T. Williams to people going into the ministry, mainly addressing men: 'Be careful regarding sex and money, because if there is a scandal related to either of these, God will forgive you but the people won't.'

Getting back into ministry or other roles of Christian authority after a moral failure requires two things: (1) God's forgiveness and favour, and (2) people who are willing to forgive and grant you a second chance. God's forgiveness is paramount. He can also, if he chooses, give you favour by preparing and opening the hearts of people. But if the people will not forgive and accept you, there is not much you can do about it.

This matter therefore goes to show how crucial it is to be absolutely honest and meticulous when it comes to handling money. In fact, when it comes to money and sex,

I don't think you can be too careful. Living near the edge simply isn't worth it.

A good case can be made that Jesus had more to say about money than any other subject in the Bible. So many of the parables refer to money, so many illustrations. Before the Fall in the Garden of Eden there would not have been a problem with money or financial security. All that one needed was provided without any effort. But after the Fall the man was commanded to work by the 'sweat of the brow' (Gen. 3:19). Money would not grow on trees.

One reason that Christians can be so unforgiving with regard to financial scandal in the Church is their anger that a minister, or other trusted person, could deliberately misuse money that was given by people who thought they were giving to God. The wilful mishandling of God's money is a serious, serious matter. After all, giving to the Church or a Christian ministry is perceived by most Christians as actually giving to *God*. I know that is largely what motivates me to give. I would not want to give money to a cause I thought was not honouring to God; therefore, when I am convinced that a church or Christian organisation is governed by integrity and devoted to the glory of God, I want to give all I can to them.

But when I find out that my money – which becomes the Lord's money – was deliberately misused or squandered, I am upset. And when people gave to my church (when I was a pastor), or give to my ministry now that I am retired, they expect me to be accountable for how it is spent.

The love of money is a root of all kinds of evil and, says Paul, 'some people, eager for money, have wandered from the faith and pierced themselves with many griefs' (1 Tim. 6:10). Someone can become 'eager for money' even when that person did not intend it to be that way. Far from it.

Tele-evangelists. Most readers will have heard of the various financial scandals there have been over the years with regard to tele-evangelists in the USA. Each case has been different, but what sometimes happens is this.

An evangelist can start out full of integrity and zeal for God but then realise he needs money to pay the bills, so he begins to express the need for financial help. If he appears on television, he can say, 'Our ministry will not continue without your help', and even promise things that will entice the viewers to give. What can then happen is that this same person who started out with integrity becomes preoccupied with being on television, emphasising the need to give money more than he should. He may begin to say things that he knows will ring a bell with viewers. Sometimes theological integrity is compromised. It's not that such people are deliberately preaching heresy, but they are catering to what will *bring in the money*. One prominent tele-evangelist in the USA personally told me that he had to raise 'two million dollars every three days'. That puts someone under a lot of pressure to keep the money flowing in from viewers.

When one's private lifestyle becomes lavish, and people discover it, an understandable suspicion emerges. People can quickly become disillusioned and stop giving when they find out that their money is paying for a luxury home. I am not suggesting that there is anything sinful about owning a luxury home, but when a ministry would not exist without the sacrificial giving of ordinary people, any whiff of financial scandal that emerges causes a lot of anger. This is why my namesake, R. T. Williams, could say 'God will forgive you, but the people won't' when a financial indiscretion is involved. Those in Christian ministry therefore need to be extremely judicious with God's money.

There is a verse in the Bible that says, 'Money is the answer for everything' (Eccles. 10:19), and some have tried to seize on this verse and exploit it. And yet, whatever else this startling verse means, it certainly shows that money is not unimportant! But God is the one who can give or withhold mercy when it comes to *anything* (Exod. 33:19). That includes financial blessing. I have thought for a long time that the missing element in the raising of money under the name of God is his sovereignty. The sovereignty of God refers to his right and power to do what he pleases with whomever he chooses. He can bless or withhold blessing. And if I get on television and promise you that 'God will bless you and make you rich' if you give to my ministry, I have treated God's sovereignty with contempt (even if I did not mean to).

I cautioned a friend of mine who is known to preach the 'prosperity gospel', 'Don't say, "God *will* bless you if you give to my ministry", but say, "God *may* bless you if you give" because God can *give* or *withhold* blessing.' The truth is, God can give or withhold mercy, and be absolutely just either way. But my friend so far has not listened to me. I pray he will not have a financial scandal of any kind on his hands – he means a lot to me.

But it is so easy to cross over a line when you are under pressure to keep the money flowing in. I don't think God wants *any* of his servants to be under that kind of pressure.

Perhaps the worst kind of financial scandal is promising people a physical healing if they will write in for a jar of anointed water – so long as they include a gift of a certain amount. There are enough simple and sincere people in the world who fall for this – and make the tele-evangelist rich. I am amazed that God does not smite these preachers rigid. But then I recall how patient God has been with me on other matters, so I lower my voice.

I do wonder if the angels cringe, however, when they hear some tele-evangelists talking about money and using the promise of prosperity to motivate viewers to give to their own ministry. I cannot imagine that God is pleased when we play directly on a person's *greed* (which needs no encouragement to expand) in order to get people to give to our ministry.

And yet, just as King Saul's gift of prophecy did not

immediately leave him after his being rejected by God, so do some religious leaders somehow apparently manage to bless a lot of people – and, for all I know, see some of them healed – despite their flamboyant lifestyle and lack of integrity. This is partly why we should never presume what is on God's mind regarding a particular ministry – whether it thrives and reaches millions, or is hardly known at all.

On the other hand, I anticipate more huge collapses of prominent people in the days that lie ahead. God may wait until the Final Judgement to expose most of them, but I expect to hear any day of him judging some of them here below.

I offer this advice to anybody who seeks not an earthly empire, but aspires to build a superstructure of gold, silver and gems and who does not want to be exposed by the Righteous Judge for abuse of money: *handle money as if there were a live television monitor pointing at you day and night for the whole world to see.* That, my friend, will serve to keep all of us on the straight and narrow. After all, one day all will be out in the open. 'For there is nothing hidden that will not be disclosed, and nothing concealed will not be known or brought out into the open' (Luke 8:17; 12:2; Matt. 10:26). I'm sorry, but the truth about everything will eventually come out.

Personal forgiveness and restoration

I must now ask you a hard question – a very hard question indeed: if you knew that God would not use you for Christian service again, would you still put yourself in a right relationship with him? In other words, is your only motive – really and truly – to get things right with your Lord Jesus Christ merely because you want to be back in a position of Christian leadership or looked up to by others? If so, I fear that is not sufficient. I must admit, I would sympathise with you; I cannot be sure how I would feel. But you must face the question: which means more to you, your relationship with God or being looked up to by others in the Church?

I don't mean to be unfair, but I would have to question how effective any future Christian service would be if this meant more to you – or me – than having intimacy with God. This could only mean that our relationship with the Father, the Son and the Holy Spirit would – at best – be second in our priorities. I'm sorry, but I must say that. If all a person wants is to get back to where he or she once was, being looked up to by all those around, he or she will fall yet again.

God is this person's judge – not me – and I cannot be sure how I myself would react if I got openly judged for every imprudent thing I have done. But why couldn't some of the high-profile evangelists who fell have *waited* a while, submitting to their leaders' wisdom, before going back on television? It certainly gives the impression that their personal egos meant more to them than God himself means to them. I fear they let the 'cat out of the bag' as to their true character by rejecting the verdict of those to whom they were accountable. It certainly suggests that their personal relationship with God was not primary. Crocodile tears flowing down one's cheeks after getting caught prove nothing about one's sincerity. When a certain friend of mine resented my loving caution, 'Please don't be like——', he sadly gave the impression that he had no real sense of guilt and shame over his fall. It smacked of having little, if any, desire to get to know God, but feeling only resentment that he got caught. All he really seemed to want was for things to be as they once were.

Although we will examine him in more detail later, I must say here that one of the reasons that God restored and used King David again after his grievous sin – and put him back on the throne in Jerusalem – was that David accepted responsibility and esteemed God's sovereign will above all else. He did not attempt to control his following – quite the opposite. He did not try to hold on to this following or encourage a single person to pursue him into his exile. He even said to Ittai the Gittite, 'Why should you come along with us? Go back and stay with King Absalom . . . May kindness and faithfulness be with you' (2 Sam. 15:19–20). He said to Zadok the priest, 'Take the ark of God back into the city. If I find favour in the Lord's eyes, he will bring me back and let me see it and his dwelling-place again. But if he says, "I am not pleased with you," then I am ready; let him do to me whatever seems good to him' (2 Sam. 15:25–26). When the fallen king was cursed by Shimei, who was pelting stones at him, David refused to respond. Why? '. . . for the Lord has told him to. It may be that the Lord will see my distress and repay me with good for the cursing I am receiving today' (2 Sam. 16:11–12).

This is a far cry from the way so many fallen heroes have accepted God's judgement upon them. I have seen it all too often: they complain that someone 'ratted' on them – and resent that person. They defend themselves. They are indignant that they have been exposed. Then, after a while – when they have no choice – they accept their lot. But not for long. They want to come back – *now*.

I will tell you how to recognise the man or woman whom God will use again: it is when they are like King David, as I just described, when they give up trying to hold on to things. It is when they are like Jesus, who 'made himself nothing' (Phil. 2:7). Jesus said, 'The man who loves his life will lose it, while the man who hates [loves less] his life in this world will keep it for eternal life' (John 12:25). This is the mandate given without exception to every fallen servant of God. Few, however, accept this mandate. But King David did. When I see that kind of spirit of humility that was exhibited by David, I will confidently predict, 'There is a man (or woman) God will use again.' They might even come back stronger than before.

As for money, the ability to handle it with godly fear is uncommon. This is why God allows relatively few of his servants to be wealthy. So many who are 'eager for money' even wander from the faith (1 Tim. 6:10). Jesus explicitly said that you will 'hate the one and love the other' or 'be devoted to one and despise the other. You cannot serve both God and Money' (Matt. 6:24). When you realise how Jesus warned of building up treasures on earth – and how dangerous riches are – it is truly appalling that some preachers play on people's greed to support their own ministries.

Those men and women who prize intimacy with the Holy Spirit above financial success are exceedingly rare. However, to people who esteem a close relationship with God more than they do anything else in the world, there is sometimes granted great financial blessing. Why? It is because such people can be trusted with wealth.

One of the more disquieting things about the 'health and wealth' teaching is that, even if it is unintentional, it encourages most people to want financial blessing more than a close walk with God. People don't need too much encouragement to use God to try to get what they want. If they are totally honest, it is not God himself who means most to them, but financial blessing. When I listen to some of these preachers (happily not all are like this), I hear very little exhortation to live a godly life to please the Lord, but only to get things from God. It is trying to 'use' God – he is but a stepping stone to wealth. I don't think God is pleased with this. Not that he does not want to bless us financially – he often does – but he wants money to be put in the right perspective.

People need to be taught how to handle money. But most of all they need to be taught that God himself should be their goal, not the money that he may give them.

I grant that God often appeals to our self-interest to secure the obedience he wants of us. 'Whoever sows sparingly will also reap sparingly, and whoever sows generously will also reap generously' (2 Cor. 9:6). Bring 'all' the tithes into the storehouse and God will pour out a blessing so great you won't be able to contain it (Mal. 3:10). But when verses like these are quoted over and over and over again, one cannot help but wonder if this is all that really matters!

My friend Kenny Samuel, a Church of Scotland minister, told me how hurt he felt as he watched one American tele-evangelist after another appear on the screen. He turned to his wife and said, 'If I did not know otherwise, I would think that Christianity is all about money.' One did not hear the gospel. One did not hear that Jesus died on the cross, or why he died – or why he was raised. It was one appeal after another to trust God for more 'things' here on earth. It grieved me to hear him say it because I feared he was right.

I hate to think what the end will be for ministries that have built their empires almost entirely by appealing to their own 'health and wealth' and prosperity teaching in order to get money for their work. And yet, ironically and sadly, so much of this money comes from the poorer people of the world. The Judgement Seat of Christ will reveal exactly what God thinks about this.

Do you want to get rich? If so, be very, very careful.

As I have said, I grew up in Ashland, Kentucky. I well remember a lady in my old church who was extremely poor and whose drunken husband abused her. But she had a glow on her face I will never forget. Her face radiated the glory of God. She was regarded as among the most godly people there. I myself had this impression of her. In my old church people would stand up and give their 'testimonies' – especially at the Wednesday-night prayer meetings, but sometimes on Sundays too. Her testimony stood out in my memory. She would rejoice with a sense of joy and the presence of God. I can almost see her now, waving her handkerchief. But after I went away to college and returned to Ashland some time later, I noticed what seemed to me to be an abrupt change in her appearance. She now wore the best of clothes, with exquisite make-up and jewellery that I assumed she could never afford. What was more, the radiant look was gone and there was no shine on her face. As for giving her testimony, she didn't give a testimony any more. I kept wondering, what has happened? The answer came: her husband had been killed in an accident, and his insurance policy pay-out made her independently wealthy. I was glad for her in a way, but on the other hand I was so sad that the money had apparently changed her. This did not need to happen.

Honesty with money comes more easily if money does not mean that much to you. When money means so much to you, the temptation to be less than honest and 'sail close to the wind' will be strong; sometimes that temptation may seem too great. You begin to rationalise, 'God knows I need this money at this time and nobody will know if I use it in a particular way – just this once.'

Jesus said that those who are faithful in what is least are faithful also in much, referring to money (Luke 16:10). This means that the person who is honest with pence will be honest in pounds.

I knew a businessman, John Johnson (not his real name), who was absolutely scrupulous with money. He built his business over the years through hard work and honesty. The time came for him to retire and he was approached by wealthy businessman Bill Williams (not his real name), who wanted to purchase John's company. I knew that Bill Williams did not have the best reputation for honesty and I was a little worried about John selling his business to Bill. I cautioned John. I was brought into the matter to make sure both sides were happy. But I will never forget what Bill Williams, the wealthier and shrewder businessman of the two, said about the less-experienced John Johnson, who had built his company carefully over the years. 'John's problem', said Bill, is that 'he is a nickel and dime man.' Bill Williams always wanted to do things in a rather questionable way, overlooking details, not being candid. John wanted every nickel and dime to be accounted for. Bill became very angry with John. John stuck to his guns – and won. But John came to realise that Bill's questionable reputation was justified – that Bill was hardly a man of transparent integrity. I have observed these two men since, and know both of them quite well. The honest 'nickel and dime' man is a contented man today; Bill is a broken, ill and sad person – he spends his time in and out of hospitals and hiring lawyers to fend off going to prison.

It is amazing what some people will do for money. The very soldiers who were guarding the tomb of Joseph of Arimathea on Easter morning – the nearest to examples of eye-witnesses to Jesus' resurrection that we are likely to discover – actually took money rather than tell what they knew was true! 'You are to say, "His disciples came during the night and stole him away while we were asleep" ', the chief priests commanded them. ' "If this report gets to the governor, we will satisfy him and keep you out of trouble." So the soldiers took the money and did as they were instructed' (Matt. 28:12–15).

Jesus asked an unanswerable question: 'What good is it for a man to gain the whole world, yet forfeit his soul?' (Mark 8:36).

I will repeat my advice for anybody reading these lines: handle every penny and every pound as though a television camera were monitoring your every move for the world to see. After all, an equivalent of a video replay or DVD will be played for all to see at the Judgement Seat of Christ. Count on that.

There are some, however, who excuse themselves for handling money in a questionable manner because they are so generous with others. It is like saying, 'I may not want everybody to know how I spend, how I arrange the bookkeeping and how I may not be totally careful with every penny, *but I do give away a lot of money* – this should make it all right.' Really?

If you have had a fall that came about through the handling of finances, but you want to be restored, I must lovingly ask: 'Do you still have the same old love of money and material things?' Remember: 'For everything in the world – the cravings of sinful man, the lust of his eyes and the boasting of what he has and does – comes not from the Father but from the world' (1 John 2:16).

Sexual purity

Martin Luther used to say that God uses sex to drive a man to marriage, ambition to drive a man to service, and fear to drive a man to faith. But the irony is, all three of these pursuits need to give way to a nobler motive. For example, *eros* love – physical love – is what God uses to make a man and a woman fall in love and want to get married, but *eros* is not capable of sustaining a marriage indefinitely. There is another kind of love – *agape* love (unselfish love) – which must parallel (not replace) *eros* love if that marriage is to flourish indefinitely. Therefore, what God uses to start a process in this case is not what he uses to complete it.

When men are commanded to love their wives as Christ loved the Church, the verb *agapao* is used. The love that motivated God to send his Son into the world (John 3:16) was *agape* – unselfish love. That is the kind of love that men are commanded to show to their wives. During the engagement period – or even the honeymoon phase – a jubilant husband cannot conceive how he would need a *command* to love his wife. But he finds out sooner or later!

Then comes the challenge. What will sustain a marriage ultimately is not one's physical attraction for the other, but love for God. You show *agape* love to your wife or husband not because *eros* is at work, but because you are obedient to Scripture. It is your love for God at work. A marriage will succeed when both the husband and the wife love Jesus Christ more than they love each other. Your love for God will motivate you to love your husband or wife as Christ loved the Church – and you will not commit adultery. *Agape* love is not a feeling; it is an act of the will. You don't pray about whether to show this unselfish love – you just *do it*.

'But my wife will not be submissive to me,' complains the husband. 'She is commanded to submit' (Eph. 5:22–24). Yes. But what if she doesn't? Is he now exempt from obedience to Christ? 'I cannot love her as Christ loved the Church when she does not submit to me,' the husband may say. And the wife may say, 'I will submit to my husband when I feel he loves me.'

What does one do in this dizzying merry-go-round? There is only one answer: you don't wait for the other to do his or her duty; you must become vulnerable and do what the Lord commands of you.

It is only a matter of time until we face sexual temptation. The sexual urge is physical; it is not merely an emotional, psychological or ego need. We are all born with this God-given physical desire. But it must be brought under control or it will lead to the worst kind of grief in this world.

Joseph, the favourite son of Jacob, faced sexual temptation after he was sold by his brothers to the Ishmaelites. Working for an Egyptian officer, Potiphar, Joseph had the opportunity for what might be called the perfect affair. Potiphar's wife began to flirt with Joseph. 'Come to bed with me!' she said to him day after day. 'She would not tell her husband; nobody back in Canaan would find out,' Joseph might have reasoned. What is more, Joseph might have held a grudge against God for letting all those bad things happen to him.

Joseph refused Potiphar's wife's overtures. His reason: 'How then could I do this wicked thing and sin against God?' (Gen. 39:9). Most people I know refuse sexual temptation mainly because they fear they might get caught if they give in. But Joseph's reason was that *God would know*. This might have been Joseph's finest hour – when he said *no* to Potiphar's wife. He may have been unaware of any spiritual power within. It may have been extremely hard for him. Perhaps that is why he '*ran* out of the house' (Gen. 39:12). But the angels said, 'Yes!' Joseph passed a most important test during this crucial time of preparation. He did not even know he was in preparation. He could not have known he had been earmarked to be a future prime minister of Egypt. He did not know that all that was going on in his life was the consequence of an Architect's carefully drawn plan. Had he known that God was preparing him for greatness, he might have had even further impetus to be honourable. But he did not know this.

That is the odd thing about preparation. It is often an unconscious matter; we don't know that it is *preparation* that is going on. What is happening is this: God is looking down the road for what is coming up and therefore puts things in our path to see how we will react. How we respond will determine the next step forward in God's plan for us. Testing, trial and even temptation are sooner or later in the package. Not that God directly tempts us. No. But he does test us – by allowing temptation to come. 'When tempted, no-one should say, "God is tempting me." For God cannot be tempted by evil, nor does he tempt anyone; but each one is tempted when, by his own evil desire, he is dragged away and enticed. Then, after desire has conceived, it gives birth to sin; and sin, when it is full-grown, gives birth to death' (James 1:13–15).

A significant part of preparation, then, often includes the issue of sexual temptation. God does us no favour to let us succeed without passing that test *first*. Dr Martyn Lloyd-Jones used to say to me, 'The worst thing that can happen to a man is to succeed before he is ready.' Therefore if a Christian reaches what could be called the pinnacle of success in the Church, and *then* succumbs to sexual temptation, it is tragic indeed. But if the kind of success that brings high profile is delayed until he has mastered his will, and manifests the fruit of the Spirit called 'self-control' (Gal. 5:23), then he is likely to maintain his position and not bring embarrassment to the kingdom.

But suppose you have already fallen? You may say, 'It is too late for me.' Wrong. I say: if you will prove yourself to be truly humble, non-defensive and submissive to godly authority, and be very, very patient, it indicates that God is not finished with you yet.

Who knows what greatness *you* have been destined for? I know this much, though. Sexual temptation is something we all must face and we must *pass the test* sooner or later if we are going to inherit what God has in mind for us. Until we face temptation and pass this test, we will not be fully ready for God's destiny for us.

If you have failed, then, there is still time – if true repentance is *granted* to you. In other words, if repentance is a true part of how you honestly feel. Chapter 9 of this book is devoted to this subject of repentance. We will see in more detail there that repentance is 'change of mind' (Greek: *metanoia*). Either repentance is there or it isn't. If you have to work it up, this is not a good sign. But if you have had a definite change of mind and are sorry, it indicates that repentance has been granted. I choose this word carefully because repentance is something that God *grants*. God '*granted* even the Gentiles repentance unto life' (Acts 11:18). The Greek word is *edoken*, from the verb *didomi* – it is given; it is a blessed and sovereign gift from God. Notice how Paul uses this word. 'Those who oppose him he must gently instruct, in the hope that God will grant them repentance leading them to a knowledge of the truth' (2 Tim. 2:25). The worst possible scenario in this connection is to cross over a line whereby God will no longer grant repentance so that you cannot be renewed again unto repentance (Heb. 6:4–6). Therefore when you are able to repent – which means God has given you a 'change of mind' – fall on your knees and thank him. It shows that God is still dealing with you.

Lot for some reason pitched his tent near Sodom (Gen. 13:12), which ominously sends a signal that he was setting himself up for temptation and a fall. The Bible calls him 'righteous', however, and he was eventually rescued (2 Pet. 2:7), despite having compromised in a most disgusting way (Gen. 19:8). But he was granted repentance. Jude appears to refer to Lot's rescue by Abraham: '. . . snatch others from the fire and save them . . . hating even the clothing stained by corrupted flesh' (Jude 23). This means that, having been delivered from a most terrible folly and granted repentance, we should loathe our past ways so that we disdain any connection with the temptation that we gave in to. 'Never again!' we must cry before God, man and the angels. 'Never again!' This is hating the garment spotted by the flesh – which we must do if we have fallen and want to be restored.

I have known some people who have given their testimony about their past life in such a way that I wondered if they regretted having their new life! Their descriptive references to what they were delivered from smacked of wishing they were still back in it! Hating the garment spotted by the flesh means you are *so sorry* for your folly that you now cut yourself off from your past by showing utter contempt for what you did.

You may know the story of Archbishop William Cranmer (1489–1556), who was burned at the stake in Oxford in 1556 for his stand on the Eucharist (the Lord's Supper). He once capitulated to the Roman authorities and signed a confession that he agreed with the Catholic doctrine of transubstantiation. But the truth is, he was very sorry indeed that he signed the confession. In any case, he was ordered to be burned at the stake. Witnesses say that as the flames were encircling his body he deliberately held out the very hand to the flame that had signed the confession, and watched it burn first, to show his utter sorrow for what he did. That is an illustration of hating the clothing stained by corrupted flesh. This is what Lot must have done after he was rescued. And it is what all of God's fallen servants must do if they expect to be used again.

True repentance means (1) a change of mind, and (2) being absolutely sorry for the things that you did that were against God's revealed will – the Bible.

All I am saying in this section on sexual purity is based upon the biblical premise that the *only* kind of sexual relationship that God commends is within the bonds of marriage – between a man and a woman. 'Marriage should be honoured by all, and the marriage bed kept pure, for God will judge the adulterer and all the sexually immoral' (Heb. 13:4). This means that any sexual activity outside of marriage, whether it be heterosexual or homosexual, is sin. I would define marriage as exclusively heterosexual (a sexual relationship between a man and a woman) and monogamous (marriage to one person).

This is what the Bible consistently teaches, and it has been the teaching of the Christian Church for 2,000 years. Ask any non-theological, unbiased reader to look up the relevant passages – and they will conclude, 'Yes, obviously, the Bible is against sex outside of marriage.' The reason I put it in this way is that we are now in a generation in which *theologians* sometimes make a case (or try to) that adultery can on occasion be acceptable and therefore not sinful. It has been called 'situation ethics'. Therefore what used to be called *sin* becomes legitimised. This has been done also with regard to homosexual practice. This calls to mind the ancient prophetic warning, 'Woe to those who call evil good and good evil, who put darkness for light and light for darkness' (Isa. 5:20).

So whether you quote from the Ten Commandments ('You shall not commit adultery' – Exod. 20:14), or relevant passages on homosexuality ('If a man lies with a man as one lies with a woman, both of them have done what is detestable, both of them must be put to death. What they have done is a perversion; their blood will be on their own heads' – Lev. 20:13; cf. Lev. 18:22) or the Sermon on the Mount ('I tell you that anyone who looks at a woman lustfully has already committed adultery with her in his heart' – Matt. 5:28), such passages have stood as the bench marks for biblical morality. As for homosexual practice, the New Testament is clear on this too; it is called 'perversion' in Romans 1:27 and is forbidden yet again in 1 Corinthians 6:9.

One of the saddest sexual rationales in recent years came out of the affair that US President Bill Clinton had with Monica Lewinsky. His playing at word games sent a hint out to many people, especially teenagers – even teenagers who call themselves Christians. President Clinton insisted, 'I did not have sexual relations with that woman, Miss Lewinsky.' But the *kind* of sex they had was not regarded by him as 'sexual relations'; therefore, many young people today are engaging in oral sex, yet saying they are not having 'sex'.

A prominent evangelical preacher in the UK was recently found to be involved in homosexual affairs. He resigned from the ministry and tore up all his sermons. If only he had hated his homosexual practice as much as he despised his ministry! The reformed world was shocked – as indeed were most Christians in the UK. Instead of repenting of his sin, he left his wife and three children to engage in homosexual activity – and, it seems, has spent a lot of time *defending* homosexual practice and using the Bible to back it up!

I wrote a book in 1988 called *Is God for the Homosexual?* (Marshall Pickering, answer: yes) in which I sought to demonstrate a love and tenderness towards people who have homosexual tendencies, but at the same time showed that the practice is sinful. As there are many robust heterosexual Christians who resist temptation day and night rather than grieve God, so should Christian people who are gay in orientation also be required to resist temptation. The gay person's libido is no stronger than that of the heterosexual. But since I wrote that book some twenty years ago the statistics seem to be changing. Not only are more and more people admitting to being gay, but this is found among ministers and worship groups too, whether evangelical or charismatic. That also means that Dr R. T. Williams's warning would be irrelevant for some men today going into the ministry – their temptations are not in the least bit *heterosexual*. I fear that the situation is worsening day by day. If this is not the repeat of the days of Lot (see Luke 17:28), indicating the last days, I don't know what is.

And yet Jesus was far more gracious towards sexual sin than he was towards self-righteous sin. He was far harder on the Pharisees for their self-righteousness and pointing the finger than he was on the woman found in adultery (John 8:1–11). We must never forget Isaiah's word about Jesus, that 'a bruised reed he will not break, and a smouldering wick he will not snuff out' (Matt. 12:20; cf. Isa. 42:1–4). This means that Jesus is extremely tender, compassionate and forgiving towards those who are sorry and who feel they have no hope – but who want somehow to get it right. The *slightest bit of life* and heart-cry is enough to attract our Lord's attention. We have a wonderful Saviour, one who was tempted at all points – like all of us – but without sin (Heb. 4:15). I pray with all my heart to be more and more like Jesus; that I will not be the slightest bit smug or judgemental towards any fallen servant of Christ, whether their fall be of a heterosexual or a homosexual nature.

Jesus' words in the Sermon on the Mount show that lusting in one's heart is tantamount to adultery, but many sound scholars believe that the Greek should be understood as *causing one to lust*. In other words, the words would be understood as, 'Anyone who *causes a woman to lust* has already committed adultery with her in his heart' (Matt. 5:28). This means that when a man *flirts* with a woman with the view of arousing her sexually, even if he does not sleep with her, he has already committed adultery with her in his heart. This flirting could be verbal (as in flattery) or non-verbal (as a facial expression or through a physical touch). When a man does this, even though he has not physically committed the act, he has committed adultery in God's sight. I think too that a woman should know that she also is addressed in these lines in the Sermon on the Mount; she should not dress, speak or touch a man in a manner that is expressly designed to cause him to lust. It works both ways.

As I said, the best way to keep from falling into sin is to avoid the temptation.

No sin brings disgrace upon the name of God like sexual sin. The secular press is thrilled beyond words when a Christian leader falls. They love it. They eat it up. They can't get enough of it. They can't get enough details. They will play it to the hilt hour after hour, day after day, night after night – whether through news or television comedians. Yes, it is almost entirely for carnal reasons. Not only that; many people (including Christians) are sexually jealous and they love to play 'gotcha' with those who fall.

But this does not excuse you or me when we play fast and loose with sexual temptation and when we choose to see how close to the edge we can get without crossing over. I say to you as if on bended knee: *don't be a fool!*

Dr Clyde Narramore used to say, 'Sex was not born in Hollywood, but at the throne of grace.' Yes. Sex is God's idea. But only in marriage – between a man and his wife.

6

Power

The measure of a man is what he does with
power. Pittacus (560–569 BC)

You would have no power over me if it were not
given to you from above. (John 19:11)

Man, proud man! Dressed in a little brief
authority, plays such fantastic tricks before
high heaven as make the angels weep.
William Shakespeare (1574–1616)

I stated in the last chapter that most falls in the Christian
life can be traced to a lack of propriety regarding one or
more of these three issues: money, sex or power. It may be
surprising at first to see how an impropriety regarding
power could bring about a Christian's leader's downfall.
But it comes down to the ancient warning, 'Pride goes before

destruction, a haughty spirit before a fall' (Prov. 16:18). The near equivalent verse is this: 'When pride comes, then comes disgrace, but with humility comes wisdom' (Prov. 11:2). Or take Eliphaz's word to Job, that God 'catches the wise in their craftiness' (Job 5:13; 1 Cor. 3:19).

When a leader falls from being too ambitious *for* power or too enamoured *of* power, it comes about because God allowed that leader to trip and get found out. Not everyone may recognise that it is God at the bottom of any topple from power, especially if it happens in the secular realm. But that is the way the Christian should perceive a prideful leader's fall. We would not know about King Nebuchadnezzar or King Herod had the accounts of their falls not been recorded in Holy Writ. In the case of King Nebuchadnezzar, he had begun to take himself too seriously. One day he was walking on the roof of the royal palace of Babylon and pontificated, 'Is this not the great Babylon I have built as the royal residence, by my mighty power and for the glory of my majesty?' I suspect the angels said, 'Really?' What we do know is that his fall came in moments. However, Nebuchadnezzar was also restored, and consequently gave God the glory. He learned his lesson and concluded, 'And those who walk in pride he is able to humble' (Dan. 4:30–37). This is a lesson that all Christians should know backwards and forwards.

In the case of King Herod, he gave an address, wearing his royal robes, sitting on his throne before his followers. They shouted, 'This is the voice of a god, not of a man.'

Whereas King Nebuchadnezzar repented and was restored, for some reason God sovereignly stepped in and judged Herod right on the spot. 'Immediately, because Herod did not give praise to God, an angel of the Lord struck him down, and he was eaten by worms and died' (Acts 12:21–23). The ancient word to Moses, 'I will have mercy on whom I will have mercy, and I will have compassion on whom I will have compassion' (Exod. 33:19) refers not only to the spiritual realm, but to the secular one as well.

When John F. Kennedy was asked, 'Why do you want to be president?', he answered: 'Because that is where the power is.' After his fall from grace, Richard Nixon said he mostly missed the power he had had in the White House and the things that went with it. 'I could order a helicopter and it was there in five minutes,' he said to a friend, but living in San Clemente, California, after being president was not only humbling for him, but it left him without power.

When Pontius Pilate was annoyed that Jesus did not answer his questions, he angrily retorted, 'Don't you realise I have power either to free you or to crucify you?' But Jesus replied, 'You would have no power over me if it were not given to you from above' (John 19:11). The Greek word translated 'power' here is *exousia* – meaning authority.

God is the sole origin of power, whether it be his creating the universe, the sustaining of creation, derived power (as electricity), political power, intellectual power, financial power, ecclesiastical power or spiritual power. 'No-one from the east or the west or from the desert can exalt a man. But it is God who judges: he brings one down, he exalts another' (Ps. 75:6–7). Power belongs to God. When one forgets that, he or she is in a very precarious position.

John Paul Jackson has told of his unusual experience with God – being brought before the Throne Room in heaven. He witnessed the immediate power of God. For the next three days, he says, he sat on the floor in the middle of a room, crying. He found himself feeling angry with God. He said, having witnessed the infinite power of God in heaven, 'Lord, one tiny drop of power from your little finger put on my hands to pray for the sick would empty every hospital in this town by noon today, but you do nothing about it.' John Paul felt that God gave him this response: 'If I gave you the power to do this, I would have to judge you because you are not able to cope with the adulation you would get.'

With any measure of power there will be an equivalent degree of temptation to pride. This is why God promises to exalt those who humble themselves. 'For whoever exalts himself will be humbled, and whoever humbles himself will be exalted' (Matt. 23:12). 'Humble yourselves, therefore, under God's mighty hand, that he may lift you up in due time' (1 Pet. 5:6). 'Though the Lord is on high, he looks upon the lowly, but the proud he knows from afar' (Ps. 138:6).

Therefore, when God allows any prideful person to get a high profile or attain a respectable level of power, it will follow that this person (1) will by the Holy Sprit learn humility on the job; (2) will be caught out – only to trip and fall, or (3) will be regarded as a sad, mediocre leader and not admired – even if he keeps his job. Sometimes it comes soon, sometimes it comes later. But it is only a matter of time. When Dr Lloyd-Jones said that the worst thing that can happen to a person is to succeed before they are ready, he was primarily thinking of the issues of pride and humility. Not many people can handle overnight success. The strength of a person sometimes is to be found not in how he or she copes with failure as much as in his or her ability to handle success. Or, as Pittacus put it, 'The measure of a man is what he does with power.'

A call to humility

We saw earlier that Joseph was earmarked for greatness and that he passed the test with regard to sexual temptation. So far, so good. But he would need more than that! Resisting sexual temptation isn't everything. He would have to learn how to *wait* until God's time comes. And during that period of waiting God has a way of bringing our sinfulness to the surface so we can confess our sins and turn from them.

The thanks that Joseph got for resisting the sexual overtures of Potiphar's wife was a prison sentence. 'Thanks a lot, God,' he might have said. But when we suffer because we do what is right, we are well on our way to being trusted with success. Yes, sometimes God deals with our faults and failures and secures repentance and improvement in us. We all have had to go through this. 'It is better, if it is God's will, to suffer for doing good than for doing evil' (1 Pet. 3:17). 'For it is commendable if a man bears up under the pain of unjust suffering because he is conscious of God . . . if you suffer for doing good . . . this is commendable before God' (1 Pet. 2:19–20).

I know a man who was found out for an impropriety and lost his position. He immediately accepted it as God's judgement on him. That was good. But when he talked about it with anybody later, he was adamant about how unfair it all was that he was caught and how unjust the manner of his dismissal was. He no doubt had a point. And yet his anger over the way in which it all came about seemed to many to show far more outrage than the indignation he should have felt that he sinned as he did in the first place. If only he had humbled himself under the mighty hand of God and stopped pointing the finger at those who didn't 'play fair', I would have held out enormous hope for him.

Joseph had a lot to forgive. He (1) had to forgive his brothers for their cruel betrayal and selling him to slavery; (2) had to forgive Jacob for being an unwise father, part of which was showing favouritism to Joseph; (3) had to forgive Potiphar's wife for her lie; (4) had to forgive Potiphar for believing his wife and so quickly having

Joseph put in prison; (5) had to forgive the cupbearer to the Pharaoh for forgetting to put in a good word for Joseph; and (6) might have had to forgive God – if he was bitter towards him – for allowing all this to happen to him. Many of us have had to do this – to forgive God. Not that God has ever done anything wrong. He *never* does anything wrong. 'He is the Rock, his work is perfect: for all his ways are judgement: a God of truth and without iniquity, just and right is he' (Deut. 32:4 – AV). But we must none the less forgive him in the sense that we affirm his right to do what he does and honour him for permitting what he does. Forgiving God is continuing to trust him no matter what – and not blaming him for anything bad that has happened to us, for any injustice or mistreatment he has chosen to allow.

This is one of the lessons Joseph had to learn. As soon as he interpreted the dream of the cupbearer to the king, he could not resist trying to pull strings. Knowing that this royal official would have his job back in three days, Joseph said to him, '. . . remember me . . . mention me to Pharaoh and get me out of this prison . . . I have done nothing to deserve being put in a dungeon' (Gen. 40:14–15). I opine that his Heavenly Father said, 'Dear Joseph, I wish you hadn't said that; you are going to need a couple more years.'

When Paul said that love is not 'self-seeking' (1 Cor. 13:5), I conclude that Joseph had not yet totally forgiven all the above at this stage; otherwise he would not have tried to nudge the arm of Providence as he did. When one totally forgives everybody for all injustice and hurt done to one, it produces a rest in God's sovereignty – and enables a person to let God be God and do the exalting in his own time. It is my belief, as I point out in my book *God Meant it for Good* (Kingsway Publications) that, during those two years after interpreting the cupbearer's dream, Joseph came to forgive everybody for all wrongs done to him. This was the final stage in his preparation. Once he was *ready*, God could trust him with success.

I don't mean to be unfair, but if you have fallen – and got caught for it – but remain bitter towards those who exposed you, you are not ready to return to ministry or any other Christian position of authority. And if you are spending your time angling as to how you can return, pulling strings and manipulating the providence of God, it suggests that you are self-seeking and not living in the love described in 1 Corinthians 13.

Humility comes not by seeking humility, but by totally forgiving everybody. There are no shortcuts. The essential step you must take if you are going to achieve all that God has envisaged for you – and I am believing that you will come back stronger than before – is to forgive every single person or group you believe mistreated you. If you believe that they lied *about* you, lied *to* you, were unfair, kept you from being vindicated, walked over you, broke their promise to you, have been guilty of the same thing they accused you of, did not give you a chance to explain yourself, betrayed you or stopped you from getting a second chance because they were determined to block your future usefulness, you have a brilliant opportunity to demonstrate perfect love.

Total forgiveness

Perhaps you know that I have written two books on forgiveness: *Total Forgiveness* and *Totally Forgiving Ourselves* (both published by Hodder). These two books show that (1) you need to forgive others – totally, and (2) you need to forgive yourself – totally.

I will briefly outline what you must do to be set free. It is *total* forgiveness, of both others and yourself. This means the following:

1 *You must not tell anybody 'what they did' to you*. The proof that Joseph totally forgave his brothers was that he made sure that nobody knew what they had done to him (Gen. 45:1–3). It seems that the first thing we do when somebody hurts us is to get on the phone – or find someone to talk to face to face – to tell 'what they did'. Why do we do this? To punish them. Perfect love casts out fear, and fear has to do with punishment (1 John 4:18). Among other things, this means that when we have not forgiven, we want to punish those who hurt us. The chief way we do this is to *tell what they did* to us. We want to make them pay. We cannot bear the thought that anybody

admires them. We are determined to get even – to break down their credibility so that nobody will respect them. When we embark on an enterprise like this, it is a dead give away that we have not forgiven them. We are still bent on vengeance. If you are doing this, you are not ready to be in ministry or hold a position of Christian leadership or authority. I'm sorry, but that is the way it is.

2 *You must not let them feel afraid of you or be intimidated by you.* When people have hurt you it may give you a gleeful, carnal joy that they are scared of you – that you will somehow hurt them or get even. Can you imagine Jesus being like that to somebody? *Never, never, never* allow a person to be afraid of you. This shows your insecurity; it is the mentality of a dictator who keeps his constituency in fear all the time. Joseph did his best to set his brothers free and refused to let them be afraid of him (Gen. 45:4).

3 *You must not do anything that would make them feel guilty or angry with themselves that they mistreated you* (Gen. 45:5). Perhaps you want to see the look on their faces when they are proved to have been so awful. You want others to see it. You perhaps fantasise how guilty they will feel one day. Total forgiveness does not require that they admit to their guilt; you forgive them even if they do not think they have done anything wrong. Your model is Jesus (Luke 23:34).

4 *You will let them save face*. Instead of 'rubbing their noses in it', you cover for them, you completely overlook what they did, you protect their egos and bolster their self-esteem. You say, 'They don't deserve to get such treatment.' I reply: whoever said they did? Do you deserve graciousness? Nobody does. God lets us save face. Joseph let his brothers save face when he said to them, '. . . it was not you who sent me here [by selling me to the Ishmaelites], but God' (Gen. 45:8). It was perhaps the most brilliant demonstration of total forgiveness in human history.

5 *You protect them from their deepest secrets and greatest fears*. The eleven brothers' greatest fear was that somehow their father, Jacob, would find out what they did and what really happened to Joseph. They would rather *die* than let Jacob learn what they in fact did to Joseph. Joseph knew that. It is so moving; read the account in Genesis 45:9–13 when he tells the brothers exactly what to say to their dad. Joseph writes the script for them; he will not allow them to tell Jacob what they did! So with you. When you protect your enemies from knowledge you could use to destroy them, you are beginning to get free.

6 *You must keep forgiving them as long as you live*. Total forgiveness is a 'life sentence'. That merely means that you have to keep doing it – as long as you live. It is not enough to do it *once*. You must do it today and again tomorrow.

And the day after tomorrow. Next week. Next month –
every day. Next year – every day. It is a life commitment.
You have to keep doing it, especially when the devil
reminds you of what they did. Joseph forgave his brothers
as long as he lived, even after Jacob died (when they were
so sure that Joseph would finally bring vengeance on
them). That is when he said to them, 'God meant it for
good' (Gen. 50:20).

7 *You pray for them to be blessed.* When you pray for
someone, you do not merely say, 'Lord, I commit them to
you' – that's not good enough. You pray that God will *bless*
them. 'Love your enemies and pray for those who persecute
you' (Matt. 5:44). And what if God really does bless them?
That is precisely what you prayed for God to do, so don't
be upset with him when he answers your prayer! If you
don't mean it, don't say it; but when you can say, 'Lord, I
ask you please to bless them', you are getting free – and fit
for Christian service in the Church.

Joseph was a man devoid of bitterness when he was asked
to interpret Pharaoh's dream. This is why he could be
trusted with greatness. There is nothing sadder than seeing
angry men and women scrambling for power – which they
will use for their personal, private platform if they get a
chance.

There is a wonderful principle connected to total
forgiveness: the greater the suffering, the greater the

anointing. If you have more to forgive than others, you have a potential anointing that others do not have. Instead of complaining about 'what they did' and giving the reason why you feel you have a right to be angry, you should seize what has happened to you with both hands: totally forgive them, set them free, let them off the hook, pray that they will be blessed. The result of this will be that you can be trusted with leadership and the possibility of success you never dreamed of. God has done you a singular favour by *withholding* success from you; otherwise it would have destroyed you. But when you have totally forgiven everybody for all that they did, you are fit, ready for Christian service. It will ensure that God will not let you succeed before you are ready.

The desire for power

We have observed that when the Apostle Paul said that 'godliness with contentment is great gain' (1 Tim. 6:6), he laid down a principle that can apply to sex and power as well as money. What Paul wants for us is that we should love God and his honour so much that we are not inordinately eager for money or driven to look outside of marriage for sexual or ego fulfilment. As I said, this means being content with your wife or husband and loving her/him as Christ loved the Church (Eph. 5:25ff) – which is the way forward for true godliness and anointing.

1 Timothy 6:6 therefore can be applied to the lust for power, a desire that has set the stage for the downfall of many a servant of Christ. At bottom, the desire for power is craving the honour that comes from people. There is something in so many of us that wants to make people jealous of us. So said the Preacher: 'And I saw that all labour and all achievement spring from man's envy of his neighbour. This too is meaningless, and a chasing after the wind' (Eccles. 4:4). In other words, what (far too often) drives a person to succeed? It is the thought that people will envy us – and be jealous of us; that is what often turns us on. Like it or not, that is the way we are!

I will never forget how this verse (Eccles. 4:4) gripped me one day. It was on 18 April 1988. It convicted me throughout my entire being. I wanted to argue with it – and say that this verse might apply to others, but not to *me*. But then I was forced to face some questions: why did I choose Oxford and not an American university or seminary to do a doctorate? And why did I want a doctorate in the first place? Why do I write books? Why do I have this driving ambition to write yet another? Why did a call to Westminster Chapel mean more to me than a small church in South Florida (which was also on offer)? I could go on and on and on – the list of soul-searching questions is endless.

I was shaken rigid. I felt so ashamed, so embarrassed. Was this truly *me*? Was my motive to succeed largely that I wanted to make people stand in awe of me? I fear that the answer was possibly yes. Not entirely, mind you, for I was doing my best to be led of the Holy Spirit and seek the honour that comes from God only. But Ecclesiastes 4:4 hit me between the eyes as few scriptures have done in my lifetime, and I have sought ever since to be a different kind of man.

This was about twenty years ago. I well remember how I could think of little else for days. I felt as if I were walking around without any clothes on. Was I to believe that my successes (such as they were) would be explained only in terms of my wanting to make people admire me – and have them feel envious?

Oh, of course I could say I did it for God! That would be true too. But I fear a more carnal motive was too often at the bottom of my pursuits. But I sought from that day to do something about it, if possible. This has been a quest for God's glory. But only a quest – I still have a long way to go.

Occasionally I get an invitation to return to Ashland, Kentucky, for a high-school reunion. I have not been able to attend any of them, but I fear that my motive for going would be quite wrong. I suspect that many of those who *don't* turn up are those who feel they haven't done much to be proud of since 1953, and those who *do* turn up want to be admired!

So much of what drives us to success can also be traced to the desire to please one's parents. I waited a long time before I got my own father's approval. I had wandered from my old teaching as well as my old denomination. I tried hard to compensate. In the end, what secured my father's approval more than anything else was that I was occupying G. Campbell Morgan's old pulpit – one of his heroes.

But the wish for parental approval is not the full explanation. I suspect that the greater driving force to succeed is probably traced to peer relationships – old and contemporary. We want to 'show them' what we have done, especially if they were rivals of some sort.

I will refer again to Martin Luther's interesting statement that God uses sex to drive a man to marriage, ambition to drive a man to service, and fear to drive a man to faith.

Yes, God uses ambition to drive a man to service. But the raw, naked wish to make people envious of us must eventually be changed, above all else, to become an ambition to make God proud of us – not making other people jealous of us. God may use sex to drive a person to marry; and he may use ambition to drive a person to service. But *agape* love and a love for the glory of God must then move in, or you and I will be anything but content with godliness. We will want more. And that is the recipe for downfall.

True power

The best antidote I know for conquering a lust for power is to embrace the implications of John 5:44: 'How can you believe if you accept praise from one another, yet make no effort to obtain the praise that comes from the only God?'

This question was addressed by Jesus to Jews, revealing precisely why they missed their Messiah. They *made no effort* to obtain the praise of God, but were addicted to the praise of men. They preferred the power that they *thought* would give them peace and joy and forfeited the very power that would have truly given such peace and joy.

There are therefore two levels of power: true power and earthly power. True power comes from above – the honour that comes from God only – including the power of the Holy Spirit. Earthly power comes from below: the praise that comes from people.

Therefore, when I speak of money, sex and power, I refer to the transitory, elusive pleasures that come on earth. The pleasure that comes from money is temporary, so too the excitement from sexual activity. The adulteress's 'house is a highway to the grave, leading down to the chambers of death' (Prov. 7:27). And the power that a Christian too often seeks is just as deadly. It is an ego trip that leads away from the power that could have been his or hers – had this person preferred the praise of God to that of people. Just as the Jews missed the Messiah who was offered to them, so have many in the Church missed the power that was on offer – had they sought God's praise.

The problem is, we suppose that our ambition to succeed is a love for God. Because we believe the Bible and the basic truths of the Christian faith we tell ourselves that our quest for more influence is for God's glory. This is how we deceive ourselves. We justify our drive to be more successful by saying we can 'reach more people', 'save more souls', 'get our message to the world' – such rationales being but a camouflage for the foolish ego trip we are on.

The truth is, the praise that comes from God would give more power than ever! For one thing, as I just stated, it may include the power of the Holy Spirit. The anointing would open more doors in a day than seeking earthly power would do in a year. But making an effort to obtain the praise of God means seeking the lower seat (Luke 14:7–11), refusing to vindicate ourselves, total forgiveness, meekness and the sheer *waiting* on God's timing. In a word: it is the way of the cross, the life of self-denial and the participation in the sufferings of Christ.

If you are a fallen servant of Christ but have been granted true repentance, and are gripped by what you are reading in these very lines, God can bring you back to service and use you more than you ever dreamed of. Let no one tell you that you cannot be used again. God would prefer a broken, obedient servant of Christ who has a 'past' to an upright, self-righteous Pharisee whose heart is as hard as nails. But it means self-denial, sexual purity and the abandonment of earthly power.

Godliness with contentment is great gain. How great? Godliness with contentment can result in power that defies a natural explanation, an anointing that can demonstrate what God can do with one man or woman who is totally resigned to his sovereign will and not bothered by the praise of people.

Finally, Martin Luther said that God uses fear to drive a man to faith, but sometimes God gets our attention through fear. Are you afraid? Have you been intimidated by the thought that you are 'finished'?

In his great hymn 'Amazing Grace' John Newton wrote:

T'was grace that taught my heart to fear, and grace those fears relieved.

Yes, that line referred to conversion, but when a backslider returns to the Lord he or she comes the same way to the cross. And when you realise that God has truly got your attention – and you come humbly with brokenness, truly repentant – you can claim the promise that, when it comes to a bruised reed, which you must be, 'a bruised reed he will not break' (Matt. 12:20).

I can remember being almost moved to tears up in the Bodleian Library at Oxford in 1975 when reading the Puritan Richard Sibbes's (1572–1635, 'the heavenly doctor') sermon, 'The Bruised Reed'. The thesis of his sermon was summed up in seven words: 'Art thou bruised? He calleth for thee.' This is because the bruised reed qualifies for God's special love.

Are you bruised? God calls you back. He can use you again.

7

The Mighty Fallen

How the mighty have fallen! Tell it not in Gath.
(2 Sam. 1:19–20)

In every saint there is something reprehensible.
John Calvin (1509–64)

The best of men are men at best. Anon.

Sometimes it is hard to work out why one person is restored after a fall and another isn't. Is it because some sins are worse than others? For example, King Saul disobeyed God by breaking the Law and was not restored; David broke the Law and was. As we shall see below, Saul broke the Ceremonial Law; David broke the Moral Law. And yet David's sin – certainly in some ways – seems worse than Saul's. The sins of adultery and murder seem worse than the wrong person offering a burnt offering. But there was one *big* difference between the two: David truly repented and Saul didn't.

Jonah disobeyed the word of the Lord to him but he repented and was restored. And though he was far from perfect, he was mightily used to turn away God's impending judgement upon Nineveh.

Samson let the Lord down most disgracefully, but eventually came back and managed to destroy more of Israel's enemies at the end of his life than he did in the whole of it.

This is so encouraging. When there is a genuine, uncontrived and unfeigned repentance, it shows there is hope – and that God is at work.

But why David repented and not Saul – and why people like Samson have been granted repentance in the end and others apparently have not – remains a mystery. Moreover, why are some found out – and others seem to get away with their sin? We will have to wait until the Final Judgement for the complete answer. In the meantime I appeal to Paul's glorious submission to the inscrutable and sovereign will of God: 'Oh, the depth of the riches of the wisdom and knowledge of God! How unsearchable his judgments, and his paths beyond tracing out! Who has known the mind of the Lord? Or who has been his counsellor?' (Rom. 11:33–34). Remaining in awe of this aspect of God's ways should keep us on our knees and make us profoundly thankful when we are granted true repentance.

King Saul

King Saul's initial fall came from ignoring what the books of Moses had to say about the priesthood and who was qualified to offer the burnt offerings. There are three aspects of the Mosaic Law: (1) the Ceremonial Law, how the people of Israel were commanded to worship God; (2) the Civil Law, how the people of Israel were to govern themselves; and (3) the Moral Law, the Ten Commandments. Only the priests – from the tribe of Levi – were allowed to offer burnt offerings and fellowship offerings (Exod. 32:26–29; Lev. 6:8–13). Saul came from the tribe of Benjamin and therefore had no right to do the work of the levitical priests. But he took advantage of his position as king and presumptuously offered the burnt offerings. Samuel alone was ordained to do this, but he was late in arriving and Saul became impatient.

'Bring me the burnt offering and the fellowship offerings' (1 Sam. 13:9). No one apparently dared to approach the king and say, 'Your majesty, with respect, you are not permitted to do this.' Saul not only took the privilege of being king too far, but he openly went against Scripture. 'You have acted foolishly,' Samuel said to him. 'You have not kept the command the Lord your God gave you; if you had, he would have established your kingdom over Israel for all time. But now your kingdom will not endure; the Lord has sought out a man after his own heart and appointed him leader of his people, because you have not kept the Lord's command' (1 Sam. 13:13–14).

But Saul was given a second chance, and yet, incredibly, he blew away the trust in him a second time! After Samuel told Saul that his kingdom would not endure, Samuel came to Saul again in 1 Samuel 15:1: 'I am the one the Lord sent to anoint you king over his people Israel; so listen now to the message from the Lord.' This should have been sweet music to Saul's ears. I would have thought Saul would seize that moment with both hands. God said to him, '. . . attack the Amalekites and totally destroy everything that belongs to them. Do not spare them; put to death men and women, children and infants, cattle and sheep, camels and donkeys' (1 Sam. 15:3). What an opportunity for Saul!

What if God were to come to *you* a second time, but require an obedience you feel is unfair and unreasonable? As we will see, either Saul did not listen carefully to what God said or he thought he would improve on God's commands! But God sometimes puts a request that seems unreasonable to us at first. God told Abraham to sacrifice Isaac; Abraham obeyed (Gen. 22). This time God was coming to Saul a second time, commanding what Saul seemed to disagree with.

My loving caution to you is this: if you have fallen – whether you are a 'layperson' or a Christian leader – but God comes to you again, take his word with *both hands*, however unfair or difficult his request seems. He wants to see if you really do want his trust.

But would you believe it – Saul disobeyed! He even justified himself for his disobedience (1 Sam. 15:20–21). Samuel said to him, 'Because you have rejected the word of the Lord, he has rejected you as king' (verse 23). That was it.

People sometimes say in competitive sport, 'It ain't over till it's over.' But for Saul it *was* now over. The anointing was *gone*.

Hebrews 6:4–6

In my book *The Anointing* (Hodder), I described Saul as a type of 'yesterday's man'. The most extraordinary thing is, even though the Lord rejected him and even departed from him (1 Sam.18:12), Saul lived on and held to the kingship for another twenty years. King Saul is an example of one who remains in a high-profile job or ministry but has none the less lost the anointing of God's favour. This is amazing. Saul *remained* king although God said to Samuel, 'I have *rejected* him as king over Israel' (1 Sam. 16:1). Why did God let him live? All I know is, God lets some survive even though they cannot ever be renewed again to true repentance.

It is impossible for those who have once been enlightened, who have tasted the heavenly gift, who have shared in the Holy Spirit, who have tasted the goodness of the word of God and the powers of the coming age, if they fall away [Greek: 'having fallen away'] to be brought back to repentance. (Heb. 6:4–6)

I am aware that this is a difficult passage. I can safely tell you that I have studied this passage more than any other in the Bible. It has been a threat to Calvinists (who teach that you cannot fall away), since this verse talks about those who have indeed fallen away. It is a threat to Arminians (who teach that you can be restored after falling away), since this verse says you cannot be brought back to repentance. I believe that this passage refers to people who have truly been saved, but are no longer granted the ability to repent of their sins.

Saul was an example of what is described in Hebrews 6:4–6. The writer describes those who fell away, but who could not be renewed *again* to repentance. Not that there had been no repentance prior to this. Quite the contrary. When the writer of Hebrews said these people cannot be renewed 'again' (Greek: *palin*, as in AV), it was because they had been granted repentance before. Indeed, they were enlightened, shared in the Holy Spirit, tasted the goodness of the word of God and the powers of the age to come (Heb. 6:4–6). They were truly converted people – as was Saul. For 'God changed Saul's heart' and even gave him the gift of prophecy (1 Sam. 10:9–12). But there came a fall – owing to unbelief – for those described in Hebrews 6 that made it 'impossible' for them to be granted repentance after that.

It is a little difficult at first to understand what entails such a fall, especially when you remember that men like Samson, David and Jonah were renewed to repentance. The answer is that they never ceased to believe God. They persevered in faith and welcomed a second chance. The Greek *parapesontas*, 'having fallen away', even if a conditional warning to the rest of the Hebrew Christians was implied, shows that these people described in Hebrews 6:4–6 had already fallen. This aorist participle comes from *parapipto*. This is a verb from the same family of words also used in Revelation 2:5: 'Remember the height from which you have *fallen*! Repent and do the things you did at first. If you do not repent, I will come to you and remove your lampstand from its place.' This shows that the use of *parapipto* or *ekpipto* (as in Rev. 2:5) does not etymologically indicate that repentance could not follow such a fall. So what exactly had these people described in Hebrews 6:4–6 done that warranted an inability to be renewed again to repentance?

The answer is: unbelief. The result of such unbelief was that they became stone deaf to the Holy Spirit. The context of this sobering passage in Hebrews 6 is Hebrews 5:11: these Hebrew Christians had become 'dull of hearing' (AV). The Greek means that they became, spiritually, 'hard of hearing'. The writer had warned of the danger that these Hebrew Christians could *repeat* (rather than repent of) the sin of unbelief that characterised the ancient Israelites. God said, 'I was angry with that

119

generation . . . their hearts are always going astray, and they have not known my ways.' This is why the writer quoted from Psalm 95:7–11: 'Today, if you hear his voice, do not harden your hearts' (Heb. 3:7–11). Why did the writer warn these Hebrew Christians in this fashion? It is because they were already spiritually hard of hearing – but at least they could *hear*! The worst scenario would be what we would call 'stone deafness' – that is, to the Holy Spirit. It is when *inwardly* one can no longer hear God speak.

The reason, then, that those described in Hebrews 6:4–6 could not be renewed again to repentance is that they were, spiritually speaking, stone deaf. They could no longer hear God speak in their hearts. It can happen to any Christian.

This is exactly what happened to King Saul. Inwardly he became stone deaf to the Spirit. Although he wore the crown and remained king for another twenty years, he no longer had an ability to hear God, despite his gift of prophecy being intact for a while.

But why would this irrevocable, tragic, spiritual condition come upon Saul and not David – or Samson? Or Jonah? Was the sin of these Christians described in Hebrews 6:4–6 the equivalent of breaking the Ceremonial Law? Or was it more like breaking the Moral Law – committing adultery, dishonouring parents, bearing false witness, or murder? Possibly. And possibly not. All we know is, they – or at least those described in Hebrews

6:4–6 – repeated the sin of ancient Israel who could not enter God's rest (Heb. 3:11, 19).

The answer given, then, to why ancient Israel could not enter into God's rest was: unbelief. This would be the reason, at bottom, why those described in Hebrews 6:4–6 fell away.

In the case of King Saul, it is clear he did not really *believe* what Exodus and Leviticus say about levitical priests alone presenting the burnt offerings. Obviously Saul did not really *believe* what God said to him about 'totally' destroying the Amalekites.

So why did God lift his anointing of approval on Saul and let him carry on as king for another twenty years? The answer is, there is a terminal chastening that does not always end in immediate death; God merely gives one up, but lets that person live without any ability to hear him speak again. This is why they cannot repent; they do not hear God any longer.

Three kinds of chastening (disciplining)

'The Lord disciplines those he loves' (Heb. 12:6). The Greek word for disciplining or chastening (AV) means *enforced learning*. God has a way of getting our attention – to teach us a lesson. Chastening is not a case of God 'getting even'; God got even at the cross! 'As far as the east is from the west, so far has he removed our transgressions from us' (Ps. 103:12). Chastening is essentially preparation; it is because God has not finished with us yet. 'No discipline seems pleasant at the time, but painful. Later on, however, it produces a harvest of righteousness and peace for those who have been trained by it' (Heb. 12:11).

There are three kinds of chastening: (1) internal chastening – when God speaks to us through his word. That is the best way to have God discipline you – internally, through the word and the Spirit. If only we would listen! (2) external chastening – Plan B. It is when people will not listen to him when he speaks clearly. It is what happened to Jonah; he was found out and God subsequently sent the fish to swallow him up. Plan B is God making a further effort to get our attention. It is like getting caught. Being exposed. Losing everything. But one can still hear God speak. (3) terminal chastening is when it is *over*. Sometimes God brings about death, as in 1 Corinthians 11:30 (those who abused the Lord's Supper) or 1 John 5:16 (the sin that leads to premature physical death).

There are therefore two kinds of terminal chastening: (a) that which leads quickly to physical death, and (b) that which results in becoming inwardly stone deaf to the Spirit – but the person lives on. The latter was what happened to King Saul.

There are probably those with a fairly high profile in business and professional positions today – not to mention the ministry – whose gift functions but who no longer hear God. If in business, they continue to make money. If they are professionals, they do their jobs well. If in ministry, like Saul, whose prophetic gift functioned for a while, they manage to keep vast followings and supporters behind them.

But Saul had irrevocably become yesterday's man even though he wore the crown and had a high profile. I don't want this to happen to you or me. We also know *how* he became yesterday's man, and if *we* do not wish to become yesterday's man or woman, there are some things we need to consider. In other words, here, summed up, is precisely how Saul became yesterday's man:

1 *He put himself above the word of God*. Saul knew that a man from the tribe of Benjamin had no right to offer burnt offerings. He knew backwards and forwards that this was for a person chosen only from the tribe of Levi – and no other. He knew exactly what he was doing when he said, 'Bring me the burnt offering.' Everybody at the time knew what the Law said about the priesthood and offering sacrifices. No one would dare do what Saul actually did. But he fancied that, since he was king, God made him an exception. Big mistake.

The best recipe I know for how to become yesterday's man or woman is to regard yourself as an exception to the rule. This is one of the devil's favourite ploys in bringing a person down. 'God understands your own situation, temperament, weakness and strengths; he does not expect you to adhere to rules like most people,' Satan says. 'You are tired, you are very important to God, he would not embarrass you or your family or allow one to hurt his own name. He knows you have needs that are different from others'.' The result is, people who listen to the devil put themselves *above* the word of God rather than *under* it. Sooner or later – surprise, surprise – they fall.

2 *He took himself too seriously.* As I said above, Saul carried the privileges of being a king too far by assuming he could do Samuel's job.

We must never forget that no one can do everything, and we all have our limits. Saul promoted himself to the level of his incompetence, going *outside* his prescribed anointing. God never promotes us to the level of our incompetence, neither does he lead us to do what we are not called to do. It is our pride – and greed – that takes us outside the limits of our gifting and calling.

It is very humbling to accept the limits of your anointing. You have to come to terms with your own degree of gifting, intelligence, strength, talent and place. You may want another's anointing, another's job, another's pulpit, another's personality, another's ability to preach or write. But God made you as you are and he does not like it when you try to be what you aren't.

A person who takes himself or herself too seriously always wants the credit. Perhaps Saul was even *glad* that Samuel was late in coming to offer the burnt and fellowship offerings. It gave him a chance to show that Samuel was not essential to Israel's life and that he, Saul, could do what Samuel could do. People like this want all the limelight; they want recognition. Undue significance. Proper respect. Special treatment. They are often among those who 'succeed' before they are ready.

3 *He felt 'compelled' to do what he did.* Justifying himself for doing Samuel's job, Saul said he 'felt compelled to offer the burnt offering' (1 Sam. 13:12). Can you believe it? *Compelled*?

Imagine that. He felt under some kind of constraint to do what was right against the revealed will of God – Scripture. Have you ever known of someone who said they felt 'led' to do what is unbiblical? Have you heard about someone who said, 'God told me to do this', even though it is without any scriptural warrant whatsoever?

One of the fastest ways to become yesterday's man or yesterday's woman is to put yourself above the word of God and then claim that 'God' has told you to do this.

Here is a good rule of thumb to remember until you die: the same Holy Spirit who wrote the Bible will not lead you contrary to what he has already said in his infallible word. Dr Martyn Lloyd-Jones used to say that the Bible was not given to replace the miraculous or immediate revelation; it was given to correct abuses. But one thing you can count on: the Holy Spirit will not contradict his inerrant word.

If you claim God has told you something when he hasn't, do not be surprised that you can carry on. He may not strike you down dead; he may not even let you be exposed. Instead he quietly and silently withdraws the anointing of his approval – and allows you to continue as if nothing has happened. This brings us to that statement I quoted in my book *The Anointing* (Hodder): 'If the Holy Spirit were completely withdrawn from the church today, ninety per cent of the work of the church would carry on as if nothing had happened.'

4 *He was accountable to nobody*. He was *supposed* to be accountable – to Samuel. But he did not listen to Samuel. To whom are you accountable? Do you think you are so close to God and so mature in wisdom and so perfect in your grasp of his will that you don't need the loving counsel and rebuke of a friend? 'Faithful are the wounds of a friend' (Prov. 27:6 – AV).

It is safe to say that most people who have a moral failure have this in common: they are not accountable to anybody who will tell them what they need to hear. To be accountable you have to (1) submit to those who know all about you and are unafraid of you; (2) listen to their rebukes and heed them; (3) do nothing in secret that they do not know about, and do nothing you know they would disapprove of. We all need someone to whom we will be accountable, people who are not afraid to tell us what we need to hear and who are aware of all our secret activities.

'I'm accountable to God,' says the person who is on the brink of a great crash. I have seen it over and over again.

Do not be surprised to learn that nearly all those who have a fall also said, 'I am accountable only to God.'

My friend Jack Taylor and I pleaded with the well-known man with the unusual prophetic gift (to whom I referred above) when I was still at Westminster Chapel. This man seemed to listen with eagerness to Jack and me as we pleaded with him. We knew – or even suspected – nothing of any sin in his life. I simply said to him, 'You are accountable to no one that we know of. You are supposed to be accountable to me, but you're not. And I fear that if you don't listen to Jack and me, you will become yesterday's man.'

The news of his fall came three years later.

5 *He was consumed by jealousy and threatened by David's anointing*. David killed Goliath and became a hero overnight. The problem was, the women came out from all the towns of Israel to meet King Saul with singing and dancing: 'Saul has slain his thousands, and David his tens of thousands' (1 Sam. 18:6–7).

Oh dear. What a pity they said that. Be careful not to take too seriously the compliments that come to you unexpectedly out of the blue. They could make you take yourself too seriously, and if jealous people hear about them, they might turn on you. What followed in the case of Saul and David was predictable. 'Saul was very angry; this refrain galled him. "They have credited David with tens of thousands," he thought, "but me with only thousands.

What more can he get but the kingdom?" And from that time on Saul kept a jealous eye on David' (1 Sam. 18:8–9).

Jealousy is the easiest thing to see in others, but often the hardest to see in ourselves. We all hate to admit to jealousy; it reveals our insecurity, and we don't like to admit to that either.

Beware of your jealous feelings. Pray to God that he will give you objectivity about yourself and cause you to see if what is at the bottom of your feelings is jealousy. It is typical of the sin that precedes a person's becoming yesterday's man or woman.

6 *He lost all sense of integrity*. Saul stooped so low that he would not even keep an oath to his own son!

What Hebrews 6:18 calls 'two unchangeable things', namely, the promise and the oath, refer to two ways in which God deals with us. A promise is usually presented upon conditions. I will do this *if you will do that*. An oath is stronger than a promise. To swear an oath, one swears by a 'greater' – in order to be believed. 'I swear by my mother's grave,' some might say in order to be believed. The oath 'puts an end to all argument'(Heb. 6:16). If you swore an oath in ancient times, the person to whom it was sworn believed it absolutely. It was the one time you knew you could trust what was said.

Saul actually swore an oath to his son Jonathan that he would not kill David. Saul even swore by the living God: 'As surely as the Lord lives, David will not be put to death'(1 Sam. 19:6). But he broke his word shortly afterwards (1 Sam. 19:9–10).

Character is immeasurably more important than gifting. It is our character – integrity – that will matter at the Judgement Seat of Christ. You and I won't be judged on how well we did our jobs, how much money we made, or how well we preached, wrote or administered our particular gift. It comes down to one thing: integrity.

7 *He apparently repented, and it seemed sincere, but it did not last.* First, Saul appeared to repent to his son Jonathan. Second, he even repented before David. When he realised that David had a perfect opportunity to kill him – but didn't – 'Saul said, "Is that your voice, David my son?" And he wept aloud. "You are more righteous than I," he said. "You have treated me well, but I have treated you badly . . . may the Lord reward you for the way you treated me today" ' (1 Sam. 24:16–19). But Saul continued to try to kill David (1 Sam. 26:1ff). And yet again, when David could have finished Saul off in one stroke, but didn't, Saul said, 'I have sinned. Come back, David my son. Because you considered my life precious today, I will not try to harm you again. Surely I have acted like a fool and have erred greatly' (1 Sam. 26:21). It was not a genuine repentance, and David knew Saul would not give up (1 Sam. 27:1).

When Jack Taylor and I pleaded with our friend to come clean and become accountable, he wept like a child. I was so encouraged, but within two weeks I knew he had not changed after all. When I heard of his downfall three years later, I immediately thought of the way Saul repented – which seemed so sincere at the time.

This 'repentance' was not the change of mind that God grants to his servants who walk in the light. It is a temporary change of heart that seems real, but doesn't last. A person may seem sorry and you might think he or she has been granted repentance after all, but it may be merely the kind of repentance that Judas Iscariot showed when he knew it was too late (Matt. 27:3–4).

8 *He sank to such depths that he participated in the very thing he had condemned.* As king of Israel, Saul had outlawed all mediums and spiritists from the land (1 Sam. 28:9), but at the end of his life he actually consulted the witch of Endor in order to get in touch with the deceased Samuel. It was then that he finally acknowledged what had been true for so long: 'God has turned away from me. He no longer answers me, either by prophets or by dreams' (1 Sam. 28:15).

This is what happens to many fallen people – they indulge in the very sin they so loudly condemn.

I am not saying that anybody whose weakness matches any of the above examples *always* becomes yesterday's man or woman. But these eight propositions should give us pause for thought and could, if we take them seriously, help to prevent our walking in the footsteps of King Saul.

More disappointing heroes in Scripture

It is encouraging to me that most of God's sovereign vessels have some blemish on their lives. Not all of those I refer to in this section would necessarily be called 'fallen', but, as John Calvin said in his commentary about Jephthah (Judg. 11), 'In every saint there is something reprehensible'.

Noah, Abraham, Isaac and Jacob. Noah became drunk on one occasion and became extremely vulnerable as a result (Gen. 9:20).

Abraham was a man who could tell lies out of fear (Gen. 12:12–13; 20:2), not to mention his unwarranted haste to make good God's promises to him by sleeping with Hagar (Gen. 16:3).

Isaac repeated Abraham's pattern of lying (Gen. 26:7) and was deceived by his appetite for a good meal (Gen. 27:4–31).

Jacob was the consummate deceiver and manipulator, a horrible father and husband, and almost always filled with self-pity (as I show in my book *Totally Forgiving Ourselves*).

Judah. One of Jacob's twelve sons, Judah was exceptionally callous. As Dr Michael Eaton put it, 'It all makes perfectly plain that God's plans go forward by his taking sinners and using them without being put off by their wickedness and brutality.' God used Rahab the harlot in one of the most pivotal epochs in Israel's history (Josh. 2; Heb. 11:31). As for Judah, he had been a man with a well-known tendency towards immorality and with a harsh, uncompassionate spirit; a man who cared nothing for his brother Joseph or his daughter-in-law, Tamar. When Tamar was found to be unexpectedly pregnant, Judah had only one thing to say: let her be burned (Gen. 38:24). He did not know that he himself was the father. She was widowed and wanted to have children. She pretended to be a prostitute, setting a trap for Judah, and he slept with her. When she became pregnant, she proved that Judah was the father (Gen. 38:13–26).

God used this to bring about a great change in Judah's life. It was Judah who pleaded for mercy for his father, Jacob, when the brothers faced the Egyptian prime minister – not knowing it was their brother, Joseph. Judah even offered himself as a substitute who would suffer in the place of Benjamin if the prime minister would release Benjamin. Judah was in distress over the thought of further suffering coming upon their elderly father, Jacob. Judah's speech before the prime minister is one of the most eloquent, impassioned examples of intercession in all Holy Writ (Gen. 44:18–34). He became a type of Jesus in his plea before the prime minister. Judah was a changed man; a sinner became a saint! What is more, all of these happenings in the life of Judah led to God's choice of him as the tribe of the Son of David. Of all the tribes of Israel, it was Judah who was chosen to be the royal line, leading to our Lord Jesus Christ.

Moses. At the age of forty, when it came into Moses' heart to visit his fellow Israelites, Moses committed murder. If that is not a *fall*, I don't know what is. He grew up knowing he was a Hebrew. Obviously God was dealing with him, and when Moses could take it no longer he decided to identify with his fellow Hebrews. He watched them at their hard labour, seeing an Egyptian beating a Hebrew. 'Glancing this way and that and seeing no-one, he killed the Egyptian and hid him in the sand' (Exod. 2:11–12). But the next day Moses found out that there were witnesses to his actions. In the New Testament, Stephen says that he thought that his own people would realise that God was using him to rescue them, 'but they did not' (Acts 7:23–25).

The event forced Moses to flee. All ties with the palace of Pharaoh were severed for ever, and Moses was a wanted man. At bottom, however, was his choice to be mistreated, along with the people of God, 'rather than to enjoy the pleasures of sin for a short time. He regarded disgrace for the sake of Christ as of greater value than the treasures of Egypt, because he was looking ahead to his reward' (Heb. 11:25–26).

Moses would have to wait a long time before he was used by God. After all, murder is not exactly the sort of thing one wants on one's record. But the fact that Moses was used of God and became the greatest figure of the Old Testament ought to encourage all of us to know that God can use anyone. But you might have to wait a good while before you can be accepted.

Never forget too that Moses did not get to enter the Promised Land. He should have known better, but he foolishly struck the rock with his rod rather than speak to it as God told him to. God is no respecter of persons. Moses was severely reprimanded by God and was not allowed to go to Canaan (Num. 20:7–12).

Even the great Moses was human like the rest of us.

Aaron. While Moses was in communion with God on Mount Sinai, Aaron showed himself to be reprehensibly weak. Giving in to the people's wicked request, 'Come, make us gods who will go before us', Aaron told them to take off their earrings and made them into a gold calf (Exod. 32:1–4). The people 'sat down to eat and drink and got up to indulge in revelry' (verse 6). Aaron maintained his place in God's ancient levitical system, but was never trustworthy.

Gideon. Known as one of the great stalwarts of faith (he earned a place in the great 'faith chapter' of the Bible – Hebrews 11:32), Gideon led Israel to victory over their ancient enemies – the Midianites – when all seemed utterly hopeless (Judg. 7). But his life ended under a cloud; he did not end very well. Gideon requested that he be given a share of the plunder from one of the battles, namely gold earrings. The weight of the gold rings came to 1,700 shekels. He should have known better, but Gideon made the gold into an ephod, which he placed in Ophrah, his town. 'All Israel prostituted themselves by worshipping it there, and it became a snare to Gideon and his family' (Judg. 8:27). And that is not all. 'No sooner had Gideon died than the Israelites again prostituted themselves to the Baals' (Judg. 8:33). It is not a very happy ending – or legacy – to an illustrious life of a true man of God. In every saint there is something reprehensible.

Jephthah. Neville Chamberlain is remembered mainly for one thing: his failure to recognise Adolf Hitler for who he was. Richard Nixon will be remembered for Watergate, Bill Clinton for his sexual weaknesses. And Jephthah, one of the most powerful men ever to emerge in Israelite history, will always be known for his foolish vow. It eclipsed the victory that won him a place in Hebrews 11:32. Jephthah promised God that, if he would truly defeat the enemy, he would give God a human sacrifice – the first person he met at his house. It was a silly, sad and needless thing to do. But he made a vow – which had to be kept. God gave Jephthah the victory, but the first person he met in his house afterwards was his own daughter (Judg. 11:30–40).

Samson. Samson is famous for being the strongest man that ever lived. But it was not a natural strength; it was supernatural – there was no doubt about that (see Judg. 14:5–20; 15:1–5, 14–15). However, he had a weakness – women. Delilah begged Samson to reveal the secret of his strength. He refused for a while, but she held out and in the end he told her that his secret was never having his hair cut. When he was asleep, she cut his hair off. He woke up, unaware that his anointing had left him (Judg. 16:20), but as weak as a child. The Philistines seized Samson, gouged out his eyes, and took him to Gaza. The future seemed hopeless, but Samson's hair began to grow and at the very end of his life he was given his old anointing and 'killed many more when he died than while he lived' (Judg. 16:30).

It is my hope, although it is very faint as I write these lines, that the man to whom I have obliquely referred in this book will be a Samson. I literally pray for this every day. If God could restore Samson, even though it was done under tragic conditions, he can restore anybody.

Eli. Dr Lloyd-Jones and I used to talk about Eli, a man who hardly earned a place in Hebrews 11. 'But I always thought there was something authentic about him,' Dr Lloyd-Jones used to say; 'I felt sorry for him.' A powerful priest in his day, Eli took young Samuel under his wing. It was to his credit that he recognised that God was dealing powerfully and unmistakably with the boy Samuel (1 Sam. 3). Eli's awful blemish on his life was that he allowed his wicked sons to carry on without doing anything about it. He knew how his sons desecrated the sacrifices and how they slept with the women who served at the entrance to the Tent of Meeting. He gave them a slap on the wrist – but little more (1 Sam. 2:22–25). It was God's will to 'put them to death' (verse 25); they died in battle (1 Sam. 4:11). It was not so much hearing that his sons were killed in battle that jolted Eli, but hearing that 'the ark of God has been captured'. Immediately he fell off his chair and died (1 Sam. 4:17–18). Despite his weaknesses, Eli somehow maintained a respect for the ark and this is what seemed to matter most to him in the end.

Hezekiah. A king of Judah at the age of twenty-five, Hezekiah 'did what was right in the eyes of the Lord, just as his father David had done' (2 Chron. 29:2). He got rid of idolatry in Israel, purified the temple, and celebrated Passover as it had not been done in years (2 Chron. 30:26). 'There was no-one like him among all the kings of Judah, either before him or after him' (2 Kings 18:5). Hezekiah did 'what was good and right and faithful before the Lord his God. In everything that he undertook in the service of God's temple and in obedience to the law and the commands, he sought his God and worked wholeheartedly' (2 Chron. 31:20–21). But there came a time when his heart was 'proud and he did not respond to the kindness [of God] shown him'. But Hezekiah repented of his pride (2 Chron. 32:25–26). He saw a wonderful deliverance from the threat of Sennacherib, king of Syria, and God also extended Hezekiah's life by fifteen years (2 Kings 20). All this points to a king who truly loved God.

But I have always had a sinking, uneasy feeling about the way Hezekiah's life ended. He unwisely showed the king of

Babylon everything in his palace, whereupon Isaiah prophesied that everything in his palace would be carried off to Babylon and 'some of your descendants, your own flesh and blood who will be born to you, will be taken away'. That to me is a pretty awful thing to look forward to. But Hezekiah's reaction to this? 'The word of the Lord you have spoken is good', he replied. For he thought, 'There will be peace and security in my lifetime' (Isa. 39:8). It is written that 'God left him to test him and to know everything that was in his heart' (2 Chron. 32:31). Though he loved God, what was also in his heart was pride and selfishness.

Jonah. Giving a commission to go to Nineveh, God said, 'Go' and Jonah said, 'No'. Then God said, 'Really?' Jonah opted for a Mediterranean holiday instead – in Tarshish (Spain). The Lord sent a wind that was so violent that it got all the sailors' attention. They cast lots to see who on the ship had caused this. God overruled and Jonah was found out. 'Throw me overboard,' he told them, for he knew he was the reason for the storm. They did. A great fish swallowed Jonah (Jonah 1). I love the way the Authorised Version begins Jonah 2:1: '*Then* Jonah prayed'! He prayed as he had never prayed in his life. What did he pray? He asked to do the very thing he had refused to do!

What does it take to make you pray? How much do you pray? Children spell love T-I-M-E. What if that is the way that God spells your love for him? How much time do you spend in prayer? Listen to these words from Martin Luther's journal: 'I have a very busy day today, must not spend two, but three, hours in prayer.' John Wesley would not think of going out into his day without two hours on his knees. But there aren't many Luthers or Wesleys around. As a matter of interest, statistics show that the average church leader in the USA and the UK spends *four minutes a day* in prayer or quiet time. And we wonder why the Church is powerless!

There is an old song that says, 'God doesn't compel us against our will but makes us willing to go'. The fish worked. Jonah repented, pleaded, cried and promised. At the bottom of all of this, God was mercifully at work. God did not have to send the wind, but he did. He did not have to overrule the rolling of the dice of the sailors, but he did. He did not have to send a fish to swallow Jonah, but he did. And he did not have to give Jonah a second chance, but he did.

'Then the word of the Lord came to Jonah a second time: "Go to the great city of Nineveh and proclaim to it the message I give you" ' (Jonah 3:1–2). Jonah obeyed this time.

Here is my opinion: had Jonah not obeyed when God came to him the second time, he could have been given what I have called terminal chastening. In other words, alongside his external chastening – Plan B – Jonah was also given a second chance. But had he rebelled after the second chance, I suspect he could have been in the worst scenario.

God might have taken his life or Jonah might have lived. But had he lived, had he said 'no' yet again, I opine that Jonah would have been in a Hebrews 6:4–6 situation – unable to be renewed unto repentance. I would not press this too far; it is simply my opinion. Neither do I know what goes on in God's mind or a person's heart that warrants judgement so that they cannot be used again. For all I know, God might have given Jonah a third, fourth, fifth chance. I know how patient he has been with me! So I would not want to press my point of view on this too much.

But when one hears God's voice saying 'Go', it shows he or she is not stone deaf to the Spirit. One should grasp *any* clear word from God with both hands. Seize the moment!

Jonah was given a second chance and he obeyed. It was not that he was perfect, though – he was angry that his message was not vindicated. He preached that in forty days Nineveh would be overturned (Jonah 3:4), and he looked forward to seeing the destruction. But the people repented and God did not send the calamity Jonah had promised. Jonah sulked and pouted, but God was very patient with him (Jonah 4).

Therefore God gave a disobedient man a second chance. And, as I said, we find out that he was still less than perfect when you read the account (Jonah 4). I have asked, did Jonah ever learn his lesson? I think he did. After all, in telling the story he let God have the last word (Jonah 4:11).

That is the key. Let God have the last word. If God could

use Jonah after his disobedience and repentance, he can use you or me.

8

The Returning Backslider

Have mercy on me, O God, according to your
unfailing love; according to your great
compassion blot out my transgressions. Wash
away all my iniquity and cleanse me from my
sin . . . Cleanse me with hyssop, and I shall be
clean; wash me, and I shall be whiter than
snow . . . Restore to me the joy of your
salvation . . . Then I will teach transgressors
your ways, and sinners will turn back to you.

(Ps. 51)

. I've wandered far away from God; now I'm
coming home. The paths of sin too long I've
trod; Lord, I'm coming home.

William J. Kirkpatrick (1838–1921)

The title of this chapter is borrowed from the great Puritan Richard Sibbes (1572–1635), known in his day as 'the heavenly doctor'. Dr Martyn Lloyd-Jones used to talk about how two of Richard Sibbes's sermons had helped him when he was feeling extremely tired and discouraged many years before – the sermons were 'The Bruised Reed' and 'The Returning Backslider'. The former is of immense encouragement to someone who feels very weak in his or her faith; the latter was written mainly to encourage those who have fallen and to show them how willing God is to receive them back. Either one of these sermons is sweet for those who want to sense the tenderness of God towards them when they are feeling low. I want that same spirit of graciousness to govern all that I say to you. If I come across as hard and inflexible – and moralising – I will have failed. I sometimes think that if you moralise to people you can also demoralise them.

The word 'backslide' means 'to relapse into error or bad ways'. The word 'backslider' or 'backsliding' is used only in the Old Testament, mostly in the Authorised Version. 'The backslider in heart shall be filled with his own ways' (Prov. 14:14 – AV). Because the word is not specifically used in the New Testament, one can almost 'manufacture' its meaning. For example, does it refer to a truly converted person who falls into sin? Yes, in my opinion. Or could you call a person a backslider who merely makes a profession of faith, but goes back into the world? I think not, in my view, although some would call anybody a backslider who made a profession of faith and does not persevere. I do not believe that all who make a profession of faith are truly saved; therefore I would rather not use the term 'backslider' for all who make a profession of faith, but only for those who have come to saving faith in Christ.

'Backsliding' is a word used by Jeremiah and Hosea. 'Your backsliding will rebuke you' (Jer. 2:19). The New International Version generally prefers the word 'faithless' (Jer. 3:6, 8, 11, 12, 14), 'turned away' (Jer. 8:5), 'unfaithful' (Jer. 31:22, 49:4), although it translates 'Return, faithless people; I will cure you of backsliding' in Jeremiah 3:22 and 'our backsliding is great' in Jeremiah 14:7. But at the same time God declared he is 'married' to the backslider (AV), 'for I am your husband' (Jer. 3:14). Hosea promised, 'I will heal their waywardness' (Hos. 14:4 – 'backsliding' – AV).

On a scale of 1 to 10, all of us have been backsliders to some degree. If 1 refers to non-scandalous sins (e.g. hurt feelings, not praying enough, lethargy), and 10 to scandalous sins (e.g. the blatant abuse of money, sex and power), who among us has not been in a backslidden state, at least at the lower end of the scale, at some point in our pilgrimage? Although Peter does not appear to be addressing 'backsliders', there is that intriguing comment, 'For you were like sheep going astray, but now you have returned to the Shepherd and Overseer of your souls' (1 Pet. 2:25). For every sin, however great or small, is a turning away from God. After all, 'all have sinned and fall short of the glory of God' (Rom. 3:23). Coming short of

God's glory is not merely a pre-conversion activity, for 'if we claim to be without sin, we deceive ourselves and the truth is not in us' (1 John 1:8). One of my favourite hymns ('Come, Thou Fount of Every Blessing') includes this verse:

O to grace, how great a debtor daily I'm constrained to be!
Let thy goodness, Lord, like a fetter, bind my wandering heart to Thee.
Prone to wander, Lord, I feel it, prone to leave the God I love;
Here's my heart, O take and seal it; seal it for Thy courts above.

Robert Robinson (1775–90)

Although the word 'backsliding' is not found in the New Testament, the Parable of the Prodigal Son (Luke 15) surely shows, among other things, that a true child of God can go off the rails and then come back to the Lord. Our Heavenly Father loves to welcome the backslider home. We must never forget too that the older brother in this parable was indignant when the prodigal son got so much attention. I don't mean to be unfair, but a returning backslider can anticipate some older brothers and sisters in the church who may not be too welcoming!

When this present book was nearly finished, a ministerial friend of mine (who has had a fall) told me of a book that argues that a fallen person in the ministry cannot be restored. I have not read it, but he had read it almost in desperation, hoping for a word of encouragement that he could be used again. He said that the book he had read gave him no hope. It might even have demoralised him completely. I cannot imagine that an inflexible approach that gives no hope for future usefulness to fallen Christians – ministers or laymen, high-profile or unknown – could be in the spirit of Jesus.

The truth is, God can use *anybody* who has truly repented. He can open doors that would normally be closed, break down barriers that would normally preclude usefulness again, open people's hearts that had previously been cold and prejudiced. To the fallen person I say: your task is to repent fully; God's job is forgiving, restoring and opening doors. It dignifies the blood that Jesus shed on the cross that a fallen saint can be forgiven and used again.

I know a lot more than I can reveal in this book. I know of people who have fallen and repented, then have come back stronger than before. I know of others who have fallen and repented who have not attained their former heights. I know only that God is not limited should he choose to make the latter house 'greater than the glory of the former' (Hag. 2:9). We limit him by our defensiveness and lack of true repentance.

I know of divorced people who have remarried and have been used of God in a most extraordinary way. Some of them have a high profile. I think too of old Dr W. M. Tidwell, who came to my church in Ashland, Kentucky, at the age of eighty, and whose impact on me as a teenager was profound. I recall that there were those who would never accept him because he had been divorced and remarried when he was young. When I think of the hard line taken by certain ministers as I grew up – not to mention some today – I am all the more amazed to see the variety of people that God uses. Louise and I will celebrate our fiftieth wedding anniversary in 2008, and I am so indebted to God for the way he has blessed us. To those who have not been as fortunate, I say: God gives fresh beginnings. When Jesus said 'every' sin (AV – 'all manner of sin') shall be forgiven (other than the blasphemy against the Holy Spirit – Matt. 12:31), this includes divorce. God hates divorce (Mal. 2:16), but divorce is pardonable.

There is also such a thing as theological backsliding. This kind of waywardness does not get as much attention as those sins that relate to money, sex and power. But this too needs to be addressed. The Galatians had backslidden theologically and spiritually. They had been influenced by Judaisers (Jews who professed faith in Christ and required that the Law, including circumcision, be imposed on Gentiles) and imbibed much of their teaching about the Law. When Paul said, 'You have fallen away from grace' (Gal. 5:4), he was rebuking them for opting for a gospel of works rather than grace alone, and trying to win them back. We won't know until we get to heaven whether they came back to the teaching of Paul. But he was mainly referring to their doctrinal waywardness, not to their moral conduct.

However, one would have to say that theological backsliding is rooted in a spiritual condition. A person can outwardly keep the Ten Commandments and be spiritually bankrupt.

My point is this. Sometimes a Christian – layman or preacher – goes off the rails doctrinally and needs to be cautioned, if not slapped hard on the wrist. But if these Christians lapse into sheer heresy, they should not be allowed to teach or preach or allowed back into ministry or positions of Christian authority until they have repented of their error and been sorted out.

King David

The only person who is described in the Bible as a man after God's own heart (1 Sam. 13:14; Acts 13:22) had what is arguably the worst fall of any child of God described in Scripture. And yet I doubt that anybody, certainly among all the kings of Israel, loved God more than David. The psalms are replete with words that demonstrate an intense, unwavering love for the Most High God.

> *I will praise the Lord, who counsels me; even at night my heart instructs me. I have set the Lord always before me. Because he is at my right hand, I shall not be shaken.*
>
> (Ps. 16:7–8)

Though you probe my heart and examine me at night, though you test me, you will find nothing; I have resolved that my mouth will not sin . . . Keep me as the apple of your eye . . . And I – in righteousness I shall see your face; when I awake, I shall be satisfied with seeing your likeness.

(Ps. 17:3, 8, 15)

The Lord has dealt with me according to my right-eousness; according to the cleanness of my hands he has rewarded me. For I have kept the ways of the Lord; I have not done evil by turning from my God.

(Ps. 18:20–21)

May the words of my mouth and the meditation of my heart be pleasing in your sight, O Lord, my Rock and my Redeemer.

(Ps. 19:14)

Search me, O God, and know my heart; test me and know my anxious thoughts. See if there is any offen-sive way in me, and lead me in the way everlasting.

(Ps. 139:23–24)

I have quoted what is merely the tip of the iceberg from some of David's psalms. He had a deep, deep love for God, but equally a great, great fear of displeasing God – unlike anybody else I can find in the Old Testament. 'O Lord, do not rebuke me in your anger or discipline me in your wrath' (Ps. 6:1). 'I know that you are pleased with me, for my enemy does not triumph over me' (Ps. 41:11). 'Teach me your way, O Lord, and I will walk in your truth; give me an undivided heart, that I may fear your name' (Ps. 86:11).

God had been singularly good to David. He was a shepherd, chosen 'from the sheep pens' (Ps. 78:70–71), a man most unlikely to be a future king of Israel. God raised him up to kill Goliath. David became an overnight hero – that is, until the women sang, 'Saul has slain his thousands, and David his tens of thousands' (1 Sam. 18:7). Killing Goliath was in a sense the best thing that ever happened to young David, but it must be said that it was also the worst thing to happen to the young David. David's overnight success was evaporated by his becoming – also overnight – the most wanted and hunted man in Israel.

God spared David from Saul. He also spared David from killing Nabal, the churlish and small-minded husband of Abigail. Moments before David was going to get vengeance upon Nabal, Abigail interceded and kept David from doing something he would have regretted for the rest of his life. He said to her, 'May you be blessed for your good judgment and for keeping me from bloodshed this day and from avenging myself with my own hands' (1 Sam. 25:33).

When we realise how God *kept* David from getting vengeance upon Nabal and how David so consistently controlled himself, behaving himself wisely in all the days of King Saul who was determined to kill David (see 1 Sam.

24:4ff, 26:8–11), we might ask, 'Why didn't God stop David from such folly later on?' You tell me!

I know only that God made David King over Judah (2 Sam. 2:4), then King over Israel (2 Sam. 5:3). He conquered Jerusalem, something that no human being had ever done (2 Sam. 5:7). He defeated the Philistines right, left and centre (2 Sam. 5:20), and he brought the ark to Jerusalem (2 Sam. 6:17). It was as if he could do nothing wrong. He seemed invincible.

But one day he got up from an afternoon nap, and saw a very beautiful woman bathing. Her name was Bathsheba. He found out that she was married – to one of his own soldiers. What David thought would be a fleeting affair ended in a melancholy surprise – she became pregnant. This was not the news David wanted. 'No problem,' he seemed to say; David sent for Bathsheba's husband, Uriah the Hittite, to come home for the weekend that he might sleep with his wife and thus cover the adultery and identity of the real father.

It didn't work. Uriah had what Puritans might call an 'overly scrupulous conscience'. He could not bear the thought of sleeping with his wife while his fellow soldiers were at war. Uriah refused to sleep with Bathsheba, no matter how hard David tried to make it happen.

The man after God's own heart, who stated how pleased God had been with him, became not only an adulterer but also a murderer. David instructed his general, Joab, to put Uriah in the fiercest area of the battle so that he would be killed. It worked. Uriah was slain, and David seemed to have got away with it.

And he *did* get away with it – for about two years. I have often wondered what was on David's mind during those two years. Did he write any psalms? He might have done. It is amazing how one's anointing can flourish regardless of one's behaviour. Never forget that the gifts and calling of God are 'without repentance' (AV), 'irrevocable' (Rom. 11:29). In other words, David's not repenting of his sin would not have stopped his anointing from working. I do not know that David *did* write any psalms during this time; I am simply saying that he might have done. We will no doubt find out when we get to heaven!

But it was not until Nathan the prophet came to David that there was any repentance. This was the same Nathan who at first gave David permission to build the temple, then had to return to David and admit that both of them had jumped the gun. Nathan and David had mutual respect for each other, but David was not prepared for what Nathan was about to uncover. He perhaps underestimated the depth of revelation that a true prophet can have.

Some of the most haunting and sobering words in the Old Testament are these: 'But the thing David had done [namely, his adultery, cover-up and murder] displeased the Lord' (2 Sam. 11:27).

God could have overruled David and stopped him committing adultery. He could also have not allowed Bathsheba to become pregnant. God could have allowed

Uriah to sleep with Bathsheba to cover up David's paternal identity. But David ended up being a murderer as well.

It is also possible that, had David truly repented immediately after his adultery and murder, with a broken and contrite heart, God might graciously have forgiven David and let him get on with things without bringing Nathan back into his life. I would certainly not try to prove this. I would only say to you, if you have fallen but have been spared the public exposure, fall on your knees before God, confess your sin and turn from it – utterly and totally – and ask God for mercy that your sin does not become public knowledge. Who knows? If you are truly a changed man or woman, without further disciplining God may spare you from the hurt and embarrassment and sorrow you so much dread.

But God let the worst scenario happen in David's case. Remember, dear friend, if God allowed the worst possible situation to emerge with a man after his own heart, he may well allow it with you or me.

Nathan began his confrontation with King David with a parable. The gist was this: a wealthy man stole the only ewe from a poor man, then slaughtered the lamb for a special guest. David burned with anger. 'As surely as the Lord lives, the man who did this deserves to die! He must pay for that lamb four times over, because he did such a thing and had no pity!' (2 Sam. 12:5–6). Isn't it noteworthy how self-righteous and judgemental a sinner can be! We saw the same thing with Judah.

Sometimes we who have our weaknesses can pontificate loudly and eloquently to others, moralising to them, when we ourselves have a greater problem than those we are trying to preach to!

'You are the man!' Nathan had to say to David. Nathan revealed to David how good God had been to David *and* how much had been revealed to Nathan. 'I anointed you king over Israel, and I delivered you from the hand of Saul. I gave your master's house to you, and your master's wives into your arms. I gave you the house of Israel and Judah. And if all this had been too little, I would have given you even more. Why did you despise the word of the Lord by doing what is evil in his eyes? You struck down Uriah the Hittite with the sword and took his wife to be your own' (2 Sam. 12:7–9).

There was good news and bad news. The good news: God forgave David. The reason for this: David was not defensive. He did not deny his sin. He did not make excuses. He did not blame anybody. He took the total responsibility and never looked back. 'I have sinned against the Lord,' he immediately stated. Nathan replied, 'The Lord has taken away your sin. You are not going to die' (2 Sam. 12:13). This was wonderful news. It meant that, unlike King Saul, who was not granted repentance nor was he ever renewed to unfeigned repentance for the rest of his life, David was different. He was truly sorry. He prayed:

*Have mercy on me, O God, according to your un-
failing love; according to your great compassion blot
out my transgressions. Wash away all my iniquity and
cleanse me from my sin. For I know my transgressions,
and my sin is always before me. Against you, you only,
have I sinned and done what is evil in your sight, so
that you are proved right when you speak and justified
when you judge.*

(Ps. 51:1–4)

The good news, then, is that David was not only found out,
but forgiven. Very good news indeed.

The bad news: Nathan prophesied to David, '. . . the
sword will never depart from your house, because you
despised me and took the wife of Uriah the Hittite to be
your own . . . Out of your own household I am going to
bring calamity upon you. Before your very eyes I will take
your wives and give them to one who is close to you, and he
will lie with your wives in broad daylight. You did it in
secret, but I will do this thing in broad daylight before all
Israel' (2 Sam. 12:10–12).

God is no respecter of persons. The man after God's
own heart would be severely chastened and disciplined.
What would follow for the next several years was sadness
and tragedy – all coming from within David's own family.

When I was at Westminster Chapel I preached for two
years on the life of David. But when I came to the end of 2
Samuel 11, I lost heart. I announced to the deacons that I

155

was ending the series on David. It happened to be about Christmas-time, and I would be changing the sermons anyway for a couple of weeks. However, I did not intend to return to the life of David. 'Why?' they asked. I replied that I did not have the 'stomach' for it – all that was left in the life of David, beginning with 2 Samuel 12, was so discouraging. I simply did not want to preach on what I called the 'downside of David'. They accepted my decision.

But after Christmas, during the first week of January, our church had a whole day of prayer and fasting and I was not prepared for what happened to me on that day. It was as though the Lord himself came into our living-room and had a conversation with me – it went something like this: 'So you aren't going to preach any more on the life of David?' 'No,' I replied. 'Don't you know that what you are calling the "downside" of David *is where most of your people are*?' I was stunned.

I announced to the deacons the following Sunday night what I felt I had learned on our day of prayer and fasting – and that I would continue with the life of David. These men were thrilled, and the following six months or so turned out to be the most exciting part of the whole series. These sermons are now in my book entitled *The Man After God's Own Heart* (Christian Focus Publications).

I do not claim to have a prophetic gift. Rarely, if I am honest, do I feel that God gives me a word for someone. But he did this, I believe, with respect to a fallen brother whom I know well. I told him that he would have a future ministry, but it would be like the 'downside' of the life of David. He might never attain his former heights and glory, but God would use him. He broke down and wept in gratitude, and it has turned out in that precise way. This man does not have the following, support or success of his previous days, but God is using him.

All that Nathan prophesied came true. Too true. Literally true. First, the child born to Bathsheba died. Second, his son Amnon raped his sister Tamar – who confessed this to her full brother, Absalom. When David heard of this he was 'furious' (2 Sam. 13:21), but did nothing. Absalom waited two years, then killed his brother Amnon. Absalom fled to avoid the wrath of his father, King David. But eventually he returned to Jerusalem and was reunited with his father. If only that were the end of the story.

Absalom took a decision to conspire against his father, the king. He engineered a high profile before all the people at the city gate and secured a vast following. If David knew about this, he would have probably assumed that Absalom was doing a lot of good stuff – if only to show how glad he was to be back in his father's favour. But he did things that subtly undermined confidence in the king. He assured them that, if the king would not give them justice, then Absalom certainly would be there for them. It would seem that the king took the loyalty of his people for granted; he did not apparently feel a need to be in close touch with them. David had no idea that Absalom would do such a thing.

But he did. 'He stole the hearts of the men of Israel' (2 Sam. 15:6). In a most underhanded way, Absalom asked David for permission to worship the Lord in Hebron. Permission was granted, then Absalom sent secret messengers throughout the tribes of Israel to say, 'As soon as you hear the sound of the trumpets, then say, "Absalom is king in Hebron" '(2 Sam. 15:10). All went according to Absalom's plan – and according to Nathan's awesome prophecy.

The bottom line was: David was forced to flee from Jerusalem. But David knew instantly that all that Absalom did was part of God's judgement on him. He never fought it, not for a moment. He submitted to it; he did not call his following to rise up and resist Absalom. He did not try to hold on to what was rightly his – the kingship, the palace, the people of Israel as a whole.

It is here that we see a further reason why David was a man after God's own heart. He knew he had greatly grieved the Lord. He knew that God himself was behind all that was going on. He took Absalom's conspiracy with utter dignity and grace.

In a word, he did not despise the chastening of the Lord (see Heb. 12:5–11). But do not forget: God's chastening, or disciplining, is not his getting even with us. As I said, God got even at the cross (Ps. 103:12). Chastening is essentially *preparation*. God goes to great pains to discipline us because he is preparing us for what is ahead. Chastening comes because God has not finished with us yet.

God had not finished with David, but David had no way

of knowing what God might be up to. He did not fight God's judgement, though.

If you have known the chastening of the Lord, I would say lovingly to you: it's not for nothing. Whom the Lord *loves*, he chastens (Heb. 12:6). You will say: 'Did not God chasten Saul?' Yes. And God gave Saul a second chance, but he blew it.

You may say, 'But Saul was not a man after God's own heart.' And I would reply: the way to find out whether *you* are a man or woman after God's own heart is to *submit totally* to God's judgement. Do not deny what you did. Do not be defensive. Do not make excuses. Do not blame this person or that. Admit it, confess it, submit to what God is doing.

Let the 'downside of David' be your blueprint and model. Do what David did.

What exactly did David do?

1 *He did not resist God's judgement.* 'Come! We must flee, or none of us will escape from Absalom' (2 Sam. 15:14). The king set out, with his entire household following him.

2 *He did not try to amass a greater following.* When Ittai the Gittite showed up to follow David, the king tried to discourage him. 'Go back and stay with King Absalom' (2 Sam. 15:19).

3 *He accepted what was apparently the new regime.* Note: he calls his son *King* Absalom! He had no idea whether he would be back in Jerusalem – ever again.

4 *He refused to take the ark of God with him.* Zadok the priest, who was determined to stay with David, had brought the hallowed ark, symbolising the Presence of God, from Jerusalem. 'Take the ark of God back into the city,' David ordered (2 Sam. 15:25).

5 *He submitted utterly to the total sovereignty of God regarding his future.* 'If I find favour in the Lord's eyes, he will bring me back and let me see it [the ark] and his dwelling-place again. But if he says, "I am not pleased with you," then I am ready; let him do to me whatever seems good to him' (2 Sam. 15:25–26). David knew that God said to Moses, 'I will have mercy on whom I will have mercy, and I will have compassion on whom I will have compassion' (Exod. 33:19). He knew that there was nothing he could do to manipulate the sovereign will of God, and he simply bowed to it.

This is what you and I must do. I have asked myself the question, writing these lines: what if I myself were in this very situation – and found myself under the gracious but severe judgement of God? Would I react as David did? Would I? Would you? *Will* you – if this is the situation you are in as you read these lines? Will you say, 'Let him do to me whatever seems good to him'?

To put it another way, David virtually followed the advice of Paul:

Your attitude should be the same as that of Christ Jesus: Who, being in very nature God, did not consider equality with God something to be grasped, but made himself nothing, taking the very nature of a servant . . .
(Phil. 2:5–7)

Jesus did not hold on to the glory he had in heaven before the Word was made flesh. We too are told to be that way, not holding on to what is so precious to us. David did not try to hold on to his kingship. He let it go because he knew God was at work. As he put it when the evil man Shimei cursed David, and the latter did nothing in return, 'Leave him alone; let him curse, for the Lord has told him to. It may be that the Lord will see my distress and repay me with good for the cursing I am receiving today' (2 Sam. 16:11–12).

These were hard, hard days for David. As he continued up the Mount of Olives he did so 'weeping as he went; his head was covered and he was barefoot. All the people with him covered their heads too and were weeping as they went up' (2 Sam. 15:30). When we sin against God, others are affected by it too. These people very probably did not know that all that was happening was rooted in God's displeasure with David's sinful act. David knew. He was weeping for one reason, they for another; he was weeping because of his folly and the fall-out of his sin; they were weeping because they loved King David.

But there was one faint rainbow that could be traced through the rain: the power of prayer.

6 *He prayed*. Whereas he did not lift his smallest finger to defend his kingship, there was one thing David could engage in that was entirely legitimate: prayer. That is something we can all do. We turn to God and put our requests – then wait and watch him work.

David had suddenly received new information that disquieted him perhaps more than anything yet: 'Ahithophel is among the conspirators with Absalom' (2 Sam. 15:31). Losing the support of Ahithophel was devastating news. Although he was not regarded as a prophet, Ahithophel certainly had the gift of wisdom. As far as we can tell, he never got it wrong. '. . . in those days the advice Ahithophel gave was like that of one who enquires of God. That was how both David and Absalom regarded all of Ahithophel's advice' (2 Sam. 16:23). When Absalom won Ahithophel over to his side, it was a major coup, and David knew the implications of this news. What could he do?

One thing, then, was left for David to do: he prayed. 'O Lord, turn Ahithophel's counsel into foolishness' (2 Sam. 15:31). I don't know how much faith David really had when he uttered that prayer, as it seemed to be asking for the impossible. But that was all David could do.

7 He acted shrewdly when God answered his prayer. After praying as David had done, Hushai the Arkite unexpectedly showed up to support him and David seized the moment. David told Hushai that he would be a burden if he followed him around, but suggested that he return to Jerusalem; 'you can help me by frustrating Ahithophel's advice' (2 Sam. 15:33–34). That is exactly what Hushai did. Ahithophel's advice (see 2 Sam. 17:1–4) would have ensured the throne for Absalom. Ahithophel's plan was accepted, but Absalom himself suggested that they summon Hushai, 'so that we can hear what he has to say' (2 Sam. 17:5).

This was the turning point. Hushai replied to Absalom, 'The advice Ahithophel has given is not good this time,' whereupon Hushai gave counsel that was carefully designed ultimately to hand the throne back to David. Lo and behold, Absalom and all the men said that the advice of Hushai was better! 'For the Lord had determined to frustrate the good advice of Ahithophel in order to bring disaster on Absalom' (2 Sam. 17:14).

God answered David's prayer.

David's exile was temporary and he eventually returned to Jerusalem as king. At some point David wrote Psalm 51, which includes these words:

Cleanse me with hyssop, and I shall be clean; wash me, and I shall be whiter than snow. Let me hear joy and gladness; let the bones you have crushed rejoice. Hide

*your face from my sins and blot out all my iniquity.
Create in me a pure heart, O God, and renew a
steadfast spirit within me. Do not cast me from your
presence or take your Holy Spirit from me. Restore to
me the joy of your salvation and grant me a willing
spirit, to sustain me. Then I will teach transgressors
your ways, and sinners will turn back to you.*

(Ps. 51:7–13)

The reference to hyssop refers to the blood of a sacrifice, as hyssop was used to sprinkle the blood (Exod. 12:22). Any returning backslider is in need of the blood of Jesus as much as when he or she first came to the Lord.

One of the most important statements in Psalm 51, however, are these words: 'The sacrifices of God are a broken spirit; a broken and contrite heart, O God, you will not despise' (verse 17). This is the key: a broken and contrite heart. This is the reason that David could be used again. As we saw, there was brokenness from the first moment that Nathan showed David his sin. No defensiveness, no excuses, no blaming others.

What David did in committing adultery and trying to cover it up was pretty awful. In many ways, it doesn't get much worse than that. So he was found out, and forgiven, and restored.

If God could do that with David, he can do it with you and me too.

9

Repentance

Then Judas, which had betrayed him, when he saw that he was condemned, repented himself, and brought again the thirty pieces of silver to the chief priests [. . .], saying, I have sinned in that I have betrayed the innocent blood.

(Matt. 27:3–4 – AV)

Then Peter remembered the word Jesus had spoken: 'Before the cock crows, you will disown me three times.' And he went outside and wept bitterly. (Matt. 26:75)

There are two kinds of repentance: one is that of Judas, the other that of Peter; the one is ice broken, the other ice melted. Repentance unto life will be repentance in the life.

William Nevins (1797–1835)

I grew up in Ashland, Kentucky, and my first pastor was Dr Gene Phillips. His influence on me was profound. He had unusual power in the pulpit, but also extraordinary charisma when speaking to people on a one-to-one basis. This may have had a slightly negative fall-out, however. I remember so well one man in my old church – Marvin. His spiritual state seemed tied to Gene Phillips, and when Dr Phillips moved from Ashland to another church, Marvin stopped coming to church. But when Dr Phillips was invited to return to Ashland to preach, Marvin would be sitting in the front row – and was the first to go to the altar after the sermon. But his 'repentance' lasted only a few days. I remember too when we heard Dr Phillips was coming back to Ashland yet again to preach, we all said, 'Marvin will be back in church this Sunday.' Yes, there he was – in the front row. It wasn't Dr Phillips's fault, but I do question whether Marvin was ever truly converted.

On my first trip to Israel in 1969 we stayed in a hotel on the Palestinian side of Jerusalem. A very colourful Arab – called Samir – sold beads and trinkets to the people day by day as we left the hotel for the bus, and would be waiting for us when the bus returned to the hotel later in the day. With a very pleasant smile, Samir would shout out, 'Beads? Do you want to buy some beads? Jesus saves! Jesus is coming soon! Hallelujah! Do you want to buy some beads?' We knew he had picked up a bit of the 'language of Zion' after so many Christian tourists had come in and out of the area.

On the following Sunday at the Baptist church near the Old City of Jerusalem, my friend Dr Jess Moody preached. It was a wonderful morning, and Jess preached a wonderful sermon. And when Jess gave his appeal for people to come forward and receive Christ, who should come forward but Samir! We were all thrilled. Jess could already envision telling his people back home how he led a Palestinian to the Lord while in Israel. But our hearts sank when, as it turned out, Samir was first outside the door as we were leaving the church. He shouted out, 'Want to buy some beads? Jesus saves! Jesus is coming soon! Hallelujah! Want to buy some beads? Jesus saves!'

Samir had a motive for walking forward in that Baptist church. He knew more of these people would buy beads from him rather than the others who had their trinkets to sell too. I suppose he had done this many times before. There was not the slightest thought of his acknowledging that Jesus died on the cross or believing in his heart that Jesus rose from the dead – much less was there any change of mind, which is what repentance is.

There has been a type of preaching in many fundamentalist churches, particularly in the USA, that might lead a person to believe that if he or she walks forward after the sermon when the altar call is given – in front of the people, then signs a card that Jesus is his or her Saviour and Lord – and is then baptised, he or she has been converted. I'm sorry, but this sort of thing has happened to tens of thousands. True repentance – a change of mind and turning from sin – sometimes does not enter the picture at all. This is not true of all such churches, of course, but is true of too many.

Which comes first in the *ordo salutis* (order of salvation): repentance or faith? I answer: it depends on how you define repentance. If repentance is defined as 'turning from every known sin', as some Puritans put it – and that this is a prerequisite to be saved – many people would never know whether or not they were saved because they would always fear they had not repented enough! It would be an endless bondage. This is why so many in those Puritan days lacked assurance of their salvation. But if repentance means a *change of mind*, as we will see below, then it does not matter which comes first – faith or repentance. John Calvin (1509–64) put faith before repentance in the *ordo salutis* because he did not want salvation to be based on whether or not you have repented enough.

If, however, you are a fallen Christian and want to be used again, I do not think that coming back to the Lord is quite the same thing as coming to him the first time. In other words, when you come initially to Christ in faith, you are trusting wholly and only in the blood he shed to wash away your sins – for which you are sorry. Being sorry for your sins shows repentance. But when you have backslidden – especially if you have fallen in a way that brings Christ's name into disrepute – and you are earnestly wanting to be not only forgiven but used again, I would have thought that a very deep repentance indeed is vital.

This book is not designed to deal primarily with the nature of conversion or saving faith, but rather with the restoration of one who has fallen but is a true Christian. The essential ingredient that promises restoration and future usefulness is genuine *repentance*. To put it another way – speaking personally, if I myself were a serious backslider and wanted assurance that I could be used of God to the maximum possibility, I would embrace the old Puritan definition of repentance. In other words, I would want to be as sure as I know how to be sure that I had turned from every known sin. I would want this *not* for assurance of salvation, but to be as sure as possible that God would use me again.

But I would add this caution: beware of self-righteousness creeping in. When a person has fallen and comes back to the Lord, he or she sometimes develops a somewhat 'holier than thou' attitude (if you can believe it). Yes, people who have sinned greatly and receive forgiveness for some reason seem to feel a need to compensate for the wasted time away from God. They sometimes become great 'pointers of the finger'! Don't let that happen to you. Unfeigned repentance combined with meekness and humility will put you in good stead to be used again.

The thesis of this book is this: God can use any fallen Christian, but on one condition: that he or she repents. When there is a broken and contrite heart after a fall, there is hope.

True repentance is what builds a superstructure made of

gold, silver and precious stones, but the fall into sin or the failure to walk in the light is what builds a superstructure of wood, hay and straw. It is only a matter of time before the superstructure will be shown for what it is. But when someone sees his or her folly in building a superstructure that will not withstand the fire revealed at the Judgement Seat of Christ, there is something that can be done while there is time: to repent truly and honestly. As long as there is life, there is hope. But, as Richard Fuller (1808–76) put it, 'You cannot repent too soon, because you do not know how soon it may be too late.' Or, as William Nevins said, 'He that waits for repentance, waits for that which cannot be had as long as it is waited for. It is absurd for a man to wait for that which he himself has to do.'

Two Greek words for 'repentance'

There are basically two Greek words used in the Bible that may be translated 'repentance': *metanoia* and *metamelomai*. The main one is *metanoia*. It means 'change of mind' – meaning the change of *nous*, 'mind' or 'understanding'. The original Greek idea in *metanoia* was 'later knowledge', 'subsequent knowledge', often with the implication lest it be 'too late'. It is said that we all have 20/20 hindsight vision. To be granted repentance, a true change of mind, is to have 20/20 vision *now* rather than later.

In other words, to repent means to see and do *now* what

you will wish you had seen and done *later*. So if one is granted repentance, it is a marvellous mercy of a sovereign God. It is being able to do what you will be glad you did, especially when you stand before God at the Judgement Seat of Christ.

Metanoia (the noun – 'repentance') is used twenty-four times in the New Testament. *Metanoeo* (the verb – 'repent') is used thirty-four times. It was central to the message of John the Baptist (Matt. 3:2, 8, 11), was used often by Jesus (Matt. 4:17; Luke 13:3, 5, 15:7, 10) and figured prominently in the preaching of the early Church (Acts 2:38; 3:19; 17:30, 20:21, 26:20). It is said to be 'granted' to the receivers, that is, given – not what you 'work up' (Acts 5:31: 11:18, Rom. 2:4; 2 Tim. 2:25). In other words, it is either there – or it isn't. It is precisely what some could not be granted 'again', as in Hebrews 6:4–6, because they became stone deaf to hearing God's voice.

Therefore, if one is given a true *change of mind* – in time before it is too late – we have only to thank God and his undeserved mercy for this marvellous privilege. The worst scenario describes Esau, who could 'bring about no change of mind, though he sought the blessing with tears' ('he found no place of repentance' – AV – Heb. 12:17). This, however, could refer to his being unable to change Isaac's mind, and might not necessarily refer to Esau's personal inability to repent.

What is absolutely certain, in any case, is knowing that God continues to give you and me true, honest, sincere, unfeigned, genuine and real repentance – a *change of mind* that comes before it is too late, as opposed to the scenario in Hebrews 6:4–6 when repentance does not come at all. Being changed from 'glory to glory' (2 Cor. 3:18 – AV) is the same thing as being renewed unto repentance. We must prize this above all else in this world.

The second word, *metamelomai*, means 'to experience remorse'. Whereas *metanoia* implies that you have arrived at a different view of something, *metamelomai* indicates that you have a different feeling about it. This is the word used in 1 Samuel 15:35, that 'the Lord was *grieved* that he made Saul king over Israel'. It is used in Psalm 110:4: 'The Lord has sworn and will not change his mind' (cf. Heb. 7:21) – that is, he will not regret his sworn oath. However, Paul uses both *metanoia* and *metamelomai* interchangeably in 2 Corinthians 7:7–10, which shows that you must not press the distinction of these meanings too far.

Judas Iscariot

Judas, one of the twelve disciples of Jesus, is in my view a type of the apostate, not a backslider. An apostate is one who eventually turns against the Christian faith, but was never truly converted in the first place. 'They went out from us, but they did not really belong to us. For if they had belonged to us, they would have remained with us; but their going showed that none of them belonged to us'

(1 John 2:19). I define a backslider as a true Christian – a person who has been truly converted but who falls, just as King David fell. As C. H. Spurgeon would say, he falls not *off* the ship, but *on* it. I would not say this of the apostate, who never was on the ship in the first place.

One of the earliest threats to the Christian faith was Gnosticism (it comes from the Greek word *ginisko* – 'to know'). It was probably a pre-Christian philosophy that claimed a secret way of knowing, but later imbibed part of the Christian faith. The Gnostics said, 'We can make the Christian faith better with our own improvements.' They had a defective teaching of the person of Christ (mainly denying his humanity) and were *antinomian* in both theology and conduct. Antinomianism (literally 'against law') is a denial of any role of the Law in the Christian life, often leading to lawlessness and immorality. Jude largely addressed the Gnostic threat and referred to those who were 'blemishes at your love feasts, eating with you without the slightest qualm – shepherds who feed only themselves. They are clouds without rain, blown along by the wind; autumn trees, without fruit and uprooted – twice dead . . . for whom blackest darkness has been reserved for ever' (Jude 12–13). He had no doubt as to their final destiny: they were lost for ever.

Peter also refers to such people. He calls them false prophets, denying the sovereign Lord who bought them – 'bringing swift destruction on themselves' (2 Pet. 2:1). Their punishment is certain. Moreover, 'it would have been better for them not to have known the way of righteousness, than to have known it and then to turn their backs on the sacred commandment that was passed on to them' (2 Pet. 2:21). Jude says that they got into the church through the back door; they have 'secretly slipped in among you' (Jude 4).

And yet Judas got in through the front door! Jesus actually *chose* him (Matt. 10:4). I don't know why, and I don't know anybody who does know why. It *may* be because Jesus wanted to set a pattern that shows that not all who come into the Church are truly born again. Judas was never born again. Jesus said early in his ministry, 'Have I not chosen you, the Twelve? Yet one of you is a devil!' (John 6:70). Then John added that Jesus 'meant Judas, the son of Simon Iscariot, who, though one of the Twelve, was later to betray him' (John 6:71). In other words, Jesus knew from the beginning who would betray him. In his high-priestly prayer he said of the Twelve, 'None has been lost except the one doomed to destruction so that Scripture would be fulfilled' (John 17:12), referring to Judas. The Authorised Version calls him 'son of perdition' (Greek: *vios tes apoleias*). This indicates his final destiny, the same as we saw of the Gnostics above.

One further point: Judas 'repented' of his betrayal of Jesus. The Greek word here is from *metamelomai*, which the New International Version translates as 'seized with remorse'. This indicates that *metanoia* was not given to Judas. He was sorry only that he got caught, or found out.

Even if he did have a bit of a change of mind ('I have betrayed innocent blood' – Matt. 27:4), it came too late. Matthew does not dignify Judas' 'repentance' with the word *metanoia*, the word generally reserved in the New Testament for true repentance. Matthew apparently wants to make the point that Judas was sorry only that things did not work out for him, and that the knowledge of his folly came too late. Remorse is often an essential ingredient in true repentance, but such a feeling can still be short of a true change of mind.

People will certainly have a kind of change of mind in hell, but it will not be a repentance that is granted by the gracious Holy Spirit. People will certainly have remorse in hell. Judas had remorse before he died and will have remorse for ever in hell. One of the things that will make hell just that is that people will have their memories in hell. The word came to the rich man who went to hell, 'Son, remember that in your lifetime you received your good things, while Lazarus [who went to heaven] received bad things [on earth], but now he is comforted here and you are in agony' (Luke 16:25). Then the rich man had a further request, that Lazarus be raised from the dead in order to warn his five brothers that hell really exists – and keep them from going there. The rich man assumed, 'If someone from the dead goes to them, they will repent' (Greek: *metanoesousin*). But the word came back – no, it is too late. The granting of *metanoia* will not come to those on *earth* if they do not believe the Scriptures. God works through his word to bestow repentance. So if people do not repent when they hear God's word, neither will they be convinced even if one rose from the dead (Luke 16:27–31).

People will experience remorse, as Judas did, in hell.

In a word, Judas Iscariot was never converted in the first place.

Incestuous sin at Corinth

It must have grieved Paul deeply when he received word that one of his converts had indulged in a kind of immorality so horrible that it 'does not occur even among pagans' – namely, a man was sleeping with his step mother. It is hard to say which probably upset Paul more – the incestuous sin or the cavalier attitude of his converts in Corinth. 'And you are proud! Shouldn't you rather have been filled with grief and have put out of your fellowship the man who did this?' (1 Cor. 5:2).

At any rate, we have a scandalous fall of a believer in the Church. This was a truly converted man, as we will see in more detail. Paul never questions whether the man who indulged in incestuous sin was saved; he questions the way it was handled – or, one should say, not dealt with at all by the church at Corinth. Therefore Paul rolled up his sleeves, stepped in, and exercised his apostolic authority and power:

Even though I am not physically present, I am with you in spirit. And I have already passed judgment on the one who did this, just as if I were present. When you are assembled in the name of our Lord Jesus and I am with you in spirit, and the power of our Lord Jesus is present, hand this man over to Satan, so that the sinful nature may be destroyed and his spirit saved on the day of the Lord.

(1 Cor. 5:3–5)

This is very strong language. Paul said the same about Hymenaeus and Alexander (1 Tim. 1:20). When a professing Christian abuses the teaching of grace through faith, the world loves it. It dishonours the name of God, hurts the Church's reputation, and discredits the gospel. Paul would prefer that people who do this be not only thrown out of the Church, but released to the devil so that they will be destroyed and the damage done will be minimised.

Disciplining a church member is rare nowadays. I am not sure why. But when people who profess the name of Jesus lead lives that openly dishonour his name, they should be confronted. Jesus put it like this, outlining four steps (should all of these steps be needed): (1) Go to the 'brother' (a saved person) who has sinned. 'Show him his fault, just between the two of you. If he listens to you [by which Jesus means 'if he repents'], you have won your brother over.' That happy possibility would be the end of the story. No need to take it further or blab it to the world. (2) If he will not listen [that is, if he does not repent], 'take one or two others along'. The reason for this is to honour an ancient principle, that 'every matter may be established by the testimony of two or three witnesses' (Deut. 19:15). (3) Take the matter to the church (Greek: *ekklesia* – 'the called out'), the people, if this sinning brother won't listen to a group of two or three. 'Tell it to the church'. This is open discipline and should embarrass the brother. But even then, said Jesus, this open rebuke may not work. (4) Excommunicate this person from the church. 'If he refuses to listen even to the church, treat him as you would a pagan or a tax collector' (Matt. 18:17). That means he should not be treated as if he were in full harmony with the body of Christ. Let him go into the world and be utterly separated from the church.

Paul gave this advice to us when we see a fallen brother or sister. '. . . if someone is caught in a sin, you who are spiritual should restore him gently. But watch yourself, or you also may be tempted' (Gal. 6:1). I love the way the Authorised Version puts it: 'restore him in the spirit of meekness'. Having to confront a fallen brother or sister is an extremely delicate matter. It is like walking on a knife edge. The slightest wrong move could be disastrous. There is only one way, says Paul: approach such a person not with a harsh, judgemental, pointing-the-finger 'how dare you do such a thing' attitude. You consider yourself – why? Because it could happen to you too! Remember the Golden Rule: 'Do to others as you would have them do to you' (Luke 6:31).

Whenever it falls to you to approach a person who has fallen into sin, never forget that the same thing could happen to you. Even though you might not fall into the exact same sin that this man or woman has fallen into, you might fall into a rather different sin – but one that grieves the Holy Spirit just as much. Never forget that we all have feet of clay. There is not a single one of us who is exempt from sudden temptation. And Satan knows our weakness and knows how to arrange circumstances and events so that we will be most vulnerable. When you hear of *any* sin committed by another person, however disgusted you may feel at first, tell yourself, 'There go I but by the grace of God', because that is absolutely true.

When Paul ordered the Corinthians to deliver this man who committed incest to Satan, he might not have expected to see him again. As far as Paul was concerned, it was a 'done deal'. It was over. But, in the words of that well-known phrase, 'It ain't over till it's over', and we have 2 Corinthians to thank for hearing the rest of the story. We might wish there were a 2 Galatians in order to find out how things turned out there, but we will never know, as I said, until we get to heaven.

Sometimes it is not merely an individual but a church that is required to repent. Jesus noted of the church at Ephesus that they had forsaken their first love. He then said to them, 'Remember the height from which you have fallen! Repent and do the things you did at first. If you do not repent, I will come to you and remove your lampstand from its place' (Rev. 2:4–5). This church had fallen but not to the point of no return; they were given another opportunity to repent – as long as they could hear God speak! 'He who has an ear, let him hear what the Spirit says to the churches' (Rev. 2:7). Thus the church at Ephesus had not reached a Hebrews 6:4–6 situation.

In 2 Corinthians we learn four things: (1) Paul's converts at Corinth obeyed his injunction. He was relieved to hear that they did what he ordered them to do. 'For I wrote to you out of great distress and anguish of heart and with many tears, not to grieve you but to let you know the depth of my love for you' (2 Cor. 2:4). Paul was thrilled to know that they did what he asked. He adds: 'If anyone has caused grief, he has not so much grieved me as he has grieved all of you, to some extent – not to put it too severely' (2 Cor. 2:5). Paul added, 'The reason I wrote you was to see if you would stand the test and be obedient in everything' (2 Cor. 2:9).

But we learn a second thing: (2) the punishment shook this man from the crown of his head to the soles of his feet – and he repented. This was possibly unexpected news, but thrilling news. What must have turned this man around was to recognise it was a no-joke thing, that the Apostle Paul categorically and unconditionally commanded that he be thrown out of the church and delivered to Satan – never to be seen again. It is the equivalent of Jesus' advice: 'treat him as you would a pagan' (Matt. 18:17). Had there been an attached condition, 'But if you *do* repent later on, do come on back and we will welcome you', I suspect the man would have weighed his options and not been so shaken. It was the thought of *no hope* that got his attention. That was what stirred the people of Nineveh – Jonah gave them no hope whatsoever, only proclaiming that in forty days Nineveh would be destroyed (Jonah 3).

There is a third thing we learn from 2 Corinthians: (3) Paul said to take the man back into the church again. 'The punishment inflicted on him by the majority is sufficient for him. Now instead, you ought to forgive and comfort him, so that he will not be overwhelmed by excessive sorrow. I urge you, therefore, to reaffirm your love for him' (2 Cor. 2:6–8). This shows that this man *had* been granted a renewal of repentance and that he was not in a Hebrews 6:4–6 situation. It also suggests that the falling away in Hebrews 6 may not necessarily be a moral matter; the fundamental problem was that they could not hear God speak. And yet any number of sins – idolatry, immorality, grumbling, ignoring warnings from those over you, or any kind of disobedience – could lead to such stone deafness.

Finally, we learn from 2 Corinthians: (4) the importance of total forgiveness. 'You ought to forgive and comfort him, so that he will not be overwhelmed by excessive sorrow.' Then Paul adds, 'I also forgive him.' But now Paul adds an astonishing further reason for forgiving this man, however despicable his sin: 'I have forgiven in the sight of Christ for your sake, in order that Satan might not outwit us. For we are not unaware of his schemes' (2 Cor. 2: 5–7, 10–11). The Living Bible puts it like this: 'A further reason for forgiveness is to keep us from being outsmarted by Satan.' This shows how crucial it is for us to forgive those who have repented: not to do so gives Satan a certain authority he would not otherwise have. In other words, when I hold a grudge, point the finger, keep a record of wrongs and refuse to let a person off the hook, it is on my part (even if unwittingly) a beckoning for Satan to walk all over me. I do not want to do that.

We therefore have a mandate to forgive the returning backslider, but this does not mean that he or she is given a platform. It is not necessarily talking about being used again – at this point. But it *does* show how very important it is for you and me to hold out the olive branch to those who have fallen and have repented.

Our attitude to the returning backslider should be the same as that of the father of the prodigal son – and not like that of the older brother who resented the prodigal getting so much attention (Luke 15:25–30). I fear there are members of some churches who feel they have never done anything very wicked and who have so little graciousness towards a returning backslider. God hates this as much as he does the prodigal son's sin. As for the prodigal son, he was so fearful that he would never be allowed back into his father's good graces. One of the best definitions of repentance is put in the Parable of the Prodigal Son to describe the prodigal's decision to turn from his old ways and ask for his father's mercy. What made him do it? Jesus said, 'When he came to his senses' (Luke 15:17 – 'came to himself' – AV). *That is repentance.*

As one of the church fathers, Ambrose (340–97), the Bishop of Milan, put it, 'True repentance is to cease from sinning.' The father's attitude when he saw his son coming home was the opposite of what the prodigal expected. Instead of running away from him, the father 'ran to his son, threw his arms around him and kissed him' (Luke 15:20). The son said, 'Father, I have sinned against heaven and against you. I am no longer worthy to be called your son' (Luke 15:21). *That is repentance.* 'But the father said to his servants, "Quick! Bring the best robe and put it on him. Put a ring on his finger and sandals on his feet. Bring the fattened calf and kill it. Let's have a feast and celebrate. For this son of mine was dead and is alive again; he was lost and is found" ' (Luke 15:22–24). The father's attitude should be the attitude of every one of us when we see the returning backslider.

I don't mean to sound harsh, but people who are biased against returning backsliders need to have repentance granted to them as much as the sinners they tend to judge. Immorality is sin; so too is self-righteousness.

Repentance was granted to one of the thieves on the cross. Jesus was crucified between two thieves, both of whom deserved what they were getting. One of them began to hurl insults at Jesus. 'Aren't you the Christ? Save yourself and us!' (Luke 23:39). But the other criminal rebuked his fellow criminal, 'Don't you fear God', adding, 'since you are under the same sentence? We are punished justly, for we are getting what our deeds deserve' (Luke 23:40–41).

That is repentance. Repentance is saying to God, 'We are getting what our deeds deserve.' A fair definition of repentance is also *agreeing with God.* It is saying, *I was wrong. I am sorry.* In other words, it is a change of mind. The thief on the cross had been granted repentance. He then made a plea, 'Jesus, remember me when you come into your kingdom' (Luke 23:42). Jesus gave him an instant pardon and assurance of heaven: 'I tell you the truth, today you will be with me in paradise' (Luke 23:43).

St Augustine (died 430), Bishop of Hippo, made an observation that has been quoted thousands of times since. Concerning a person receiving the Lord on their death bed – right at the last moment – Augustine said, 'There is one case of death bed repentance recorded, that of the penitent thief, that none should despair; and only one that none should presume.' As Bishop Jeremy Taylor (1613–67) said:

> *It is the greatest and dearest blessing that ever God gave to men, that they may repent; and therefore to deny or to delay is to refuse health when brought by the skill of the physician – to refuse liberty offered to us by our gracious Lord.*

If God grants repentance, treat it as you would a vast fortune – of gold, silver or gems. For God's granting true repentance means an invitation to erect a superstructure that will make all the discipline you have been through worth everything at the Judgement Seat of Christ.

10

Simon Peter

'No,' said Peter, 'you shall never wash my feet.'
Jesus answered, 'Unless I wash you, you have
no part with me.' 'Then, Lord,' Simon Peter
replied, 'not just my feet but my hands and my
head as well!' (John 13:8–9)

Simon, Simon, Satan has asked to sift you as
wheat. But I have prayed for you, Simon, that
your faith may not fail. And when you have
turned back, strengthen your brothers.
(Luke 22:31–32)

I tell you the truth, before the cock crows,
you will disown me three times! Do not let
your hearts be troubled. Trust in God;
trust also in me. (John 13:38—14:1)

> Peter was hurt because Jesus asked him the
> third time, 'Do you love me?' He said, 'Lord, you
> know all things; you know that I love you.'
> Jesus said, 'Feed my sheep'. (John 21:17)

I wanted the final chapter of this book to demonstrate clearly that a fallen person can be used again, so I now write about my favourite disciple among the Twelve – the most famous and colourful of them all.

Simon Peter was a choleric, sanguine, take-charge type of person, always sticking his foot in it, devoted but unpredictable. 'Wonderfully messed up,' as Jeff Lucas put it. I am sure that under a lie-detector test, Peter honestly believed that he loved the Lord far more than *any* of the Twelve. When Peter was in the Spirit he was in the Spirit indeed – truly brilliant – but when he was in the flesh, he was in the flesh indeed – not so brilliant! I suspect many Christians identify with Peter more than they do the other disciples, even if they are not born leaders.

Peter was the unofficial spokesman for the Twelve. 'Master, we've worked hard all night and haven't caught anything. But because you say so, I will let down the nets.' (Luke 5:5). They immediately caught a large number of fish. When Peter saw this, he fell at Jesus' knees and said, 'Go away from me, Lord; I am a sinful man! ' (Luke 5:8). This shows the Holy Spirit at work, otherwise Peter would not have been conscious of his sinfulness. After that, Jesus issued the call: 'from now on you will catch men' (Luke 5:10; Matt. 4:19). But it was Andrew who initially introduced his brother Simon to Jesus – 'We have found the Messiah' – and brought him to Jesus, who looked at him and said, 'You are Simon son of John. You will be called Cephas (which, when translated, is Peter)' (John 1:42). This was reaffirmed later after Peter confessed to Jesus – one of those times he was truly led of the Holy Spirit – 'You are the Christ, the Son of the living God', and Jesus said, '. . . you are Peter, and on this rock I will build my church, and the gates of Hades will not overcome it' (Matt. 16:18).

Jesus had his inner circle – comprised of three men who were let in on events that the others apparently knew nothing about – Peter, James and John. On one of these occasions Jesus took these three to a high mountain and he was transfigured before them. His face shone like the sun, and his clothes became white. Moses and Elijah appeared on the scene, talking with Jesus. Peter said to Jesus, trying hard to impress him, 'Lord, it is good for us to be here. If you wish, I will put up three shelters – one for you, one for Moses and one for Elijah.' This was not Peter's finest hour. Then a voice came from a bright cloud that enveloped them and said, 'This is my Son, whom I love; with him I am well pleased. Listen to him!' They were terrified and fell face down on the ground. But when they were able to look up, they saw no one except Jesus – a loving rebuke from the Father that Jesus was greater than Moses or Elijah.

The same three men were allowed to witness Jesus'

raising a child from the dead (Mark 5:37–43). Peter, James and John were also singled out to share in Jesus' dark hour in Gethsemane (Matt. 26:37).

All four of the Gospels tell of Jesus' prophecy that Peter would deny him – and all four also describe the denial itself. But John's account adds a story not in the Synoptic Gospels (that is, Matthew, Mark and Luke). It was during the occasion when Jesus poured water into a basin and began to wash his disciples' feet, drying them with a towel he had wrapped around himself.

Not one of the Twelve protested about Jesus washing their feet – that is, until Jesus came to Simon Peter. Peter decided to exploit the moment to show he was different from the rest and that he loved the Lord more than the others. So when Jesus came to Peter, in order to show that he was more humble and a cut above the others, Peter asked, 'Lord, are you going to wash my feet?' It was as though he were saying, 'You don't really think I am going to let *you* wash my feet, do you?' But Jesus made it clear – yes, that is exactly what he intended to do. Jesus graciously replied to Peter, 'You do not realise now what I am doing, but later you will understand.'

At this stage Peter was feeling really proud of himself. 'No,' he said, 'You shall never wash *my* feet.' He was sending a signal to all present – not only to Jesus, but also to the eleven others, as if to say, 'These men should be ashamed of themselves for letting you wash their feet; they should be washing *your* feet.' Peter was trying hard again to impress Jesus that he loved him more than the others did – indeed, that he loved Jesus too much, respected him too much and valued his stature too much, to allow him to lower himself by washing their feet. How dare these men allow such a thing! 'No, Lord, you will never wash *my* feet.'

But Peter was soon put in his place. Jesus answered, 'Unless I wash you, you have no part with me.' That smarted a bit.

Now Peter had to come up with a good one! He needed not only to save face for his pious protest, but to outdo these less spiritual men in showing his superior love for Jesus. 'Then, Lord . . . not just my feet but my hands and my head as well!' (John 13:9).

I think this aspect of the life of Peter should send a signal to 'pious' people who want the world to know how godly they are. Should this send a signal to you and me? Perhaps you don't need this, but I have to admit that I do. It is a timely reminder that I must not ever fall into the trap of overestimating how much I love the Lord.

It is like the Elijah complex. The ancient prophet sincerely thought he alone was left – that he was the only true prophet of God (1 Kings 18:22, 19:10). Elijah was wrong – very wrong. He completely forgot about Obadiah and the hundred prophets who had risked their lives in defiance of the wicked King Ahab (1 Kings 18:4). Not only that; in due course the Lord told Elijah that he had another 7,000 in Israel who had not bowed to Baal (1 Kings 19:18). Whenever we start feeling a little bit sorry for ourselves and imagine that we are so very important to God, he has a way of putting us in our place in order to keep us from taking ourselves too seriously.

So if you are among those who like to let people know how much you love God, then, more than ever, you should keep quiet about it. We should not even tell ourselves, much less others, how devoted to the Lord Jesus Christ we may think we are. This is why Paul said that he did not even judge himself (1 Cor. 4:3). Trying to assess how much we love God by how much we give, pray or fast is the same thing as letting our left hand know what our right hand is doing (see Matt. 6:1–18).

Why? It is because a rebuke from God – one way or another – may be coming soon. And, God forbid, maybe even a grievous fall.

Jesus was getting ready to give Simon Peter the shock of his life. He was about to let Peter know that he would deny even *knowing* Jesus, but he gently prepared him for this sobering forecast. It came immediately after a dispute arose among the Twelve as to which of them was considered to be greatest. Jesus stepped in and said, 'the greatest among you should be like the youngest, and the one who rules like the one who serves' (Luke 22:26).

Peter had been right in the middle of this vehement discussion. How do we know this? Because Peter was immediately singled out. 'Simon, Simon, Satan has asked to sift you as wheat' (Luke 22:31).

How did Jesus know that Satan had asked to sift Peter as

wheat? Jesus had said, 'The Son can do nothing by himself; he can do only what he sees his Father doing, because whatever the Father does the Son also does' (John 5:19). Jesus saw what was going on in the heavenlies, when Satan had to get permission from God before he could proceed to work through Peter. 'Satan has asked.' He asked God the Father. You may recall that Job's trial was preceded by a conversation in heaven between Satan and God. Satan could do no more than God permitted (Job 1). So Jesus saw that Satan had his eye on Simon Peter. Nothing catches God by surprise, but it is interesting that all that followed – when Peter denied the Lord – was preceded by this eye-opening disclosure – namely, that Satan was behind the whole thing, but within the permissive will of God.

You should know that if you are a chosen vessel, you are also a target of Satan. Jonathan Edwards said that when the Church is revived, so is the devil. The closer you get to God, the more the devil will be aware of you.

Satan trembles when he sees the weakest saint upon his knees.

William Cowper (1731–1800)

My old friend Rolfe Barnard, now in heaven, used to preach a sermon called 'The Man Who Was Known in Hell', basing it on the account of the seven sons of Sceva who were trying to cast out devils in the name of Jesus, saying, 'In the name of Jesus, whom Paul preaches, I command you to come out.' They were actually trying to do something they were not at all qualified to do. And yet the evil spirit answered, 'Jesus I know, and I know about Paul, but who are you?' (Acts 19:15). Satan did not know these people! The point that Rolfe Barnard wanted to make is summed up in his own words: 'I want to be known in hell.' That means that Rolfe would be a threat to the devil. Unfortunately, so many Christians are no threat to the devil. Satan does not know about them! Tell me, are you known in hell? Do you think that Satan is aware of you? Are you a threat to him?

Satan was aware of Peter. And when you have a calling and mission from God, Satan will want to interfere and abort that mission. Do you think that you could be a target of Satan?

Then Jesus added four things when he spoke to Peter: (1) 'I have prayed for you'. There is nothing grander or more powerful than having the intercessory prayer of Jesus behind you. The moment Jesus said that, one could be assured of the ultimate outcome. (2) 'That your faith may not fail'. This was an implicit admission that Peter had faith, but faith can be weak and not persevere. Peter had Jesus' prayer behind him, that his faith would persevere. (3) 'When you have turned back', an implicit indication that Peter would have a fall, but also that he would be restored. Jesus knew that his prayer would be answered, that Peter's failure would be temporary. (4) 'Strengthen your brothers'. This meant that Peter would resume the kind of leadership he was known to have among the other disciples, that he would be in a position to encourage them all.

Peter immediately replied, 'Lord, I am ready to go with you to prison and to death' (Luke 22:33). Peter said that because he meant it. At Westminster Chapel we used to sing an old hymn called 'O Jesus, I have promised to serve Thee to the end'. Peter promised this.

Then came the most stunning word Peter ever heard Jesus utter: 'I tell you, Peter, before the cock crows *today*, you will deny three times that you know me' (Luke 22:34; Matt. 26:34; Mark 14:30; John 13:38). 'Today'. This seemed utterly preposterous and Peter insisted emphatic-ally, 'Even if I have to die with you, I will never disown you.' And all the other disciples said the same thing (Mark 14:31).

John's account is interesting. Keeping in mind that there were no chapters or verses in the original Greek, Jesus said to Peter, 'I tell you the truth, before the cock crows, you will disown me three times! Do not let your hearts be troubled. Trust in God; trust also in me' (John 13:38–14:1). The Greek is in the second person singular to Peter – '*you* will disown me three times' – then he addressed all of them who had said they would never disown the Lord, 'Let not your *hearts* be troubled.' Jesus lovingly included the whole lot in his compassion. In other words, Jesus not only knew what Peter would do, he knew too that 'all' the disciples would desert him and flee (Matt. 26:56).

But the point is this. In the same breath that Jesus told

Peter that he would deny him, he added, as it were, 'Don't worry!' Amazing. 'Do not let your hearts be troubled.' It is as though Jesus said to them, 'I know exactly what will happen, but it's OK – everything is under control.'

God is never *really* disappointed. Displeased? Yes. Disappointed? No. It is because he knows the future as well as he knows the past. Moreover, he does not panic.

Imagine this! Jesus knows that Peter will fall, but expresses his everlasting love the same moment. I call that *love*. When you know in advance that someone is going to let you down, but love them just the same, it is a most remarkable matter.

But Jesus is that way with us. He knows if we are going to let him down, but he loves us just the same.

The thing is, Peter didn't believe a word of it. And yet a few hours later – on the very same day – it all transpired. Jesus was betrayed by Judas, then arrested. He was taken to the high priest. A girl who was on duty asked Peter, 'You are not one of his disciples, are you?' And, would you believe it, Peter replied, 'I am not' (John 18:17). It was a cold night and Peter was warming himself by the fire. He was asked for the second time, 'You are not one of his disciples, are you?' The reply: 'I am not.' And then one of the high priest's servants challenged him, 'Didn't I see you with him in the olive grove?' (John 18:26). According to Mark's account, it was at this stage that Peter 'began to call down curses on himself, and he swore to them, "I don't know this man you're talking about" ' (Mark 14:71). The cock crowed, and as it crowed the second time, Peter remembered the words that Jesus had spoken to him. 'He broke down and wept' (Mark 14:72). 'He went outside and wept bitterly' (Matt. 26:75; Luke 22:62).

I would have thought that the guilt Peter felt at that moment was incalculable. We can only imagine what depth of sorrow and shame he felt. But it was too late. All Peter could do now was to lean on Jesus' unconditional love and trust those words that Jesus had spoken to be utterly and infallibly true.

But on Easter Sunday at the empty tomb, the angel instructed the women who came early in the day to anoint the body of Jesus, 'Go, tell his disciples *and Peter*' that Jesus would see them in Galilee 'just as he told you' (Mark 16:7). Peter was singled out in the initial message of Easter. It demonstrates the wonderful grace of God.

After Jesus was raised from the dead, ten of the disciples (Thomas was absent, Judas out of the picture) were assembled in a room behind locked doors. They were afraid that the Jews might find them. You can be sure too that they, especially Peter, were ridden with guilt. Jesus unexpectedly came and stood among them. His words were: 'Peace be with you!' The disciples were 'overjoyed' when they saw the Lord' (John 20:19–20). This joy came not only from the realisation that Jesus had been raised from the dead, but from having him appear to them without moralising or making them feel the slightest bit ashamed. He might have rebuked them and said, 'How *could* you have done this? Three years with you, and you end up deserting me! How *could* you?' However, there was not a hint of that. Their sin was pardoned so completely that it was as though they'd never sinned at all. Jesus' further word was, 'Peace be with you! As the Father has sent me, I am sending you' (John 20:21).

The disciples were reinstated on the spot.

Later on Jesus appeared on the shore of the Sea of Tiberias, then prepared breakfast for the disciples. After they had finished eating, Jesus turned to Peter and asked, 'Simon, son of John, do you truly love me more than these?' (John 21:15). I interpret this to mean that it was Jesus' way of saying to Peter, who felt so embarrassed, unlike the rest of them, 'Do you *still* think you love me more than these do?' As we have seen, Peter always took it for granted that he was the most devoted of the disciples, but this boast was taken away from him in one stroke.

As Peter disowned Jesus three times, Jesus asked Peter three times, 'Do you love me?' Peter was hurt because Jesus asked him the third time, but he shouldn't have been. When we have failed our Lord, he has every right to test us.

The most amazing thing of all, however, is this: Peter has not only been forgiven and reinstated, but was chosen to preach the inaugural sermon of the Church on the Day of Pentecost. One could ask, which would have been more surprising: that Peter would have been set aside to make room for a different disciple to preach (if only to discipline Peter further), or that the same Peter who denied knowing

Jesus only fifty days before would be chosen so soon after his denial to be in such a ministry?

Simon Peter had already taken over as leader among the eleven disciples during the waiting period in the Upper Room between Christ's ascension and Pentecost. Jesus had prayed that Peter would be able to strengthen his brothers, and Peter was perhaps starting to do this. He stood up among the believers and took the view that somebody should replace Judas (Acts 1:15–26). Whether Peter was correct in his conclusion about Judas is debatable, but we need not go into that here. But if you ask, 'How dare Peter have such confidence and authority to take the lead in this manner?', the only answer is: he knew he was a forgiven man. Jesus totally set him free by the way Peter's denial had been foretold, but also by the way Peter was given special attention by Jesus after his resurrection. So Peter was in no doubt.

Being without any doubt is what gave Peter such confidence on the Day of Pentecost. He even uses this word in his sermon: 'Brothers, I can tell you *confidently* (Greek: *parresias* – confidence, freedom, boldness) . . .' (Acts 2:29). This confidence, or boldness, is an essential part of the anointing, that phenomenon which an older generation used to call 'unction' of the Spirit. Such power flows when you know without any doubt that (1) all your sins are totally forgiven, (2) what you are saying is absolutely, objectively true, (3) you have the undoubted approval of God, (4) you are the very instrument of the Holy Spirit, saying exactly what God wants to be said and nothing he doesn't want to be said, and (5) the hearers are 'cut to the heart' as they were on the Day of Pentecost (Acts 2:37).

But there is yet another reason that Peter was so effective on the Day of Pentecost, and it is perhaps the main reason he had such power and acceptance among people. He did not have a trace of a judgemental or pompous attitude left in him; Peter's self-righteous balloon had been punctured. He also knew that he was completely unworthy to be preaching that sermon. There was no pharisaical, arrogant, pointing-the-finger, condescending spirit in his personality or presentation; he was a transparent vehicle of the Holy Spirit. When one has grievously sinned, but repented and been given infallible assurance of forgiveness, the result is, in a word, power.

I remember a particular Sunday morning in the pulpit at Westminster Chapel. I never felt so unworthy to preach in all my life. Louise and I had had a big argument in our flat just before I had to leave for church. I slammed the door and pressed for the lift. I was fuming. The next thing I know is that I am sitting on the large circular platform, bowing my head and looking spiritual. By then I had come to my senses. I thought, 'Lord, there is no way I am going to be used today. I am unfit to be preaching.' During the singing of the hymns I tried to get Louise's attention – to send a non-verbal signal to say 'I am sorry' – but she did not make eye contact with me. There was no way I could send her a note – somebody might read it. I was simply shut up to the mercy of God. I had never felt such a fraud. Never expecting for one moment to be blessed or helped in preaching, I just started quietly and slowly.

I couldn't believe what was happening. An amazing authority took over, and I had liberty such as I had not known. The thoughts flowed. There was power there – but it wasn't me.

God was able to take over and he did. I was utterly out of the picture. I couldn't get over it. I went to the vestry and, simply, thanked the Lord with a huge profuseness and gratitude. What is more, I thought of Peter when he preached at Pentecost. It came to me: 'That's it. Peter was devoid of self-righteousness and filled with unworthiness and that is why God used him, and why he used me today.' Not that I was thankful for my abysmal attitude at home. Believe me, I apologised to Louise as soon as I got home (and was forgiven). But I was grateful for the lesson. I have tried ever since not to depend on my spiritual sense of preparation, unless by that one means a feeling of absolute powerlessness and emptiness of self.

I am saying that Peter probably preached better than he would have done had he not had the embarrassing fall at the very time the Lord was being handed over to the authorities. 'All things work together for good to them that love God, to those who are called according to his purpose' (Rom. 8:28 – AV). But one of the main principles of the truth of Romans 8:28 is this: the fact that something works out for good *doesn't mean it was right at the time the less-*

than-good thing happened. God simply has a way of overruling by his grace and making things look good in the end. The good that results is the product of sheer grace, not that what we did was good or right.

Peter was a changed and new man. His fall did not keep God from using him.

Lessons from Peter's fall and restoration: things we must not conclude

We must be careful about jumping to wrong conclusions regarding Peter's fall and restoration. I will outline five things we should *not* assume about Peter's restoration:

1 *That all who fall will be used again.* The truth is, not all who fall will – or can – be used again. There are several reasons for this. First, there is the possibility that so much damage has been done through some people's falls and failure that it is not reasonable to think they can be restored to full service in the near future. Moses committed murder. There is no way God could have used him immediately after that. You will recall that Moses waited forty years before he was used.

Second, some sins *are* worse than others. The book of Leviticus goes to great lengths to show this. The New Testament teaches this as well (Luke 12:48; John 19:11). To say glibly 'sin is sin' and that one sin can be forgiven as readily as another is to speak the truth – but only up to a point. Yes, God forgives all sin (save that of the blasphemy of the Holy Spirit), but it does not follow that all situations are the same. For example, Peter's sin was reprehensible, but it was not scandalous in the sense that the name of God was put to an open shame. It is debatable whether Peter broke any of the Ten Commandments by denying he knew Jesus, although in the light of Jesus' interpretation of them he broke the third and ninth Commandments. (This would take a considerable time to explain.) The point is, there is no hint of scandal or shame in Peter's denial for which the Law would demand punishment. Moreover, Peter's failure was probably known only to a few and would possibly have been forgotten had not the four Gospels called attention to it.

2 *That those who will be used again need to wait only fifty days after their failure.* The shortness of time between Peter's failure and his remarkable preaching on the Day of Pentecost has been used by some as a reason they 'don't need to wait two years' – or whatever time others perceive as being appropriate. First, it is hard to believe that a person is sincere in his or her repentance if they expect to be used so soon – especially if they *demand* to be used!

Second, when we have failed the Lord Jesus Christ through bad behaviour we have in that moment forfeited any 'right' – if we ever really had one – to be used by him after that. We should never, ever forget this. We lose any right to represent God after we have let him down. All we can do is ask for forgiveness; it is up to him whether – or when – we are used again. Anyone 'snapping their finger' towards God, and expecting God to salute him or her from the heavenlies smacks of not knowing God or his ways at all. It is therefore ludicrous – silly – to use the fifty-day time period as a pattern for how long a person should wait before they are brought back into ministry or Christian service.

3 *That those who fall should not have to worry about further disciplining.* It could be argued by some that Peter did not undergo any discipline at all for his denial of Christ. There was no judicial court, panel or committee that passed judgement on Peter. And when Jesus appeared to him after the resurrection, there was no hint that Peter ought to be disciplined before he be launched into ministry.

My answer to this is that ecclesiastical structures had not been set up at this time. Peter's failure came before there was any time or need for church government as such. It is dishonouring to God to bypass the godly opinions of those whose responsibility it is to look after the Church and the honour of God's name.

4 *That those who fall will not have to face the consequences of their sin.* First of all, Peter faced the consequence of what he did the moment he heard the cock crow and saw the look of the Lord straight at him. He sobbed his heart

out. He would have given a thousand worlds not to have done what he did. He would have to live with that for ever. And yet his denial of Jesus did not result in the horrendous kind of hurt and sorrow that comes to a spouse, family, church or community as a result of, say, sexual sin.

Second, the fact that God forgives our sin is no hint that we do not have to live with the consequences of our sin. God forgave David. But not only did the child die who had been born to Bathsheba, but the endless sorrow in David's heart from the happenings among David's family continued on and on for years. We all have to live with the consequences of what we have said and done even though our sins have been washed away by the blood of Jesus Christ.

5 *That those who fall and are restored will be exalted overnight.* It is true that Peter was restored and exalted within a very few days. Yes, he became the most talked-about figure in Jerusalem for a good while, but this is owing to the circumstances of the day, which are not likely to be repeated. God can do anything, but there are some things he will not do during your lifetime or mine: he will not make two and two equal five, or make a rock so big he cannot lift it. We all have to live within the perimeters of the society into which we have been born and which we must reach.

Lessons from Peter's fall and restoration:
things we may conclude

1 *All who fall can be forgiven.* Never forget that good old promise, 'If we confess our sins, he is faithful and just and will forgive us our sins and purify us from all unright-eousness' (1 John 1:9). It cannot be stressed enough that *all* manner of sin and blasphemy (except the blasphemy of the Holy Spirit) is pardonable.

Peter's being forgiven is encouragement to us all. Take the matter of witnessing to the lost. Have you ever failed to witness to a lost person because you feared what the reaction of that person or other people might be? This could be the very equivalent of Peter's sin. God will forgive you for this. Not only that; he forgives the worst possible sins – all those that come under the scrutiny of the Ten Commandments. Sins against the Ten Commandments are *all* forgivable.

Jesus will not break the bruised reed. I suspect that Jesus felt just as keenly and deeply for Peter as Peter felt for himself when the crowing of the cock was heard. I would not press this too far, but perhaps it hurt Jesus as much as it hurt Peter – just to have to watch Peter weep as he did.

2 *We are all loved with an everlasting love.* What was true of ancient Israel is true of every born-again child of God: 'I have loved you with an everlasting love' (Jer. 31:3). Jesus never stopped loving Peter in all he did. There was nothing

Peter could have done to make Jesus love him more, and nothing he could have done to make Jesus love him less. We are loved with an everlasting, perfect and unconditional love.

3 *God is still married to the backslider.* When God rebuked Israel for her waywardness and backsliding, he still said, 'I am your husband' (Jer. 3:14). That has not changed; we are the bride of Christ. God hates divorce (Mal. 2:16) and practises what he preaches! Since we are the bride of Christ, God is determined to present us faultless in the end (Eph. 5:27; Jude 24). In the meantime, he rebukes and chastens us (Rev. 3:19).

If God is the husband, he is the head – and provider. He will look after us in every detail.

4 *God can use anybody.* I say this fully aware that God can overrule every principle I am outlining in this very chapter. I have given my cautions, but obviously God is not bound by anything I say in this book, no matter how much I want to be (and hope I am) led by Scripture.

Church history is riddled with exceptional cases and unusual people – who seem to break all the rules. I myself resisted being ordained for a long time because my hero Charles Haddon Spurgeon was never ordained. He said: 'Their empty hands on my empty head will not add to my empty ministry.' But one day I had a stark revelation – I'm not Spurgeon! So I submitted to ordination.

If there is any message I would be pleased to convey, and

be remembered for most of all, it is this: God can use anybody. If he could use Peter, Moses, Jonah, David, Judah or Gideon, he can use me. And, believe me, dear reader, if God can use me, he can use anybody.

5 *All who anticipate being used again must repent as sorrowfully as Peter did.* Peter did not weep bitterly because he knew cameras were focused on him, or because he thought this scene would be written up and remembered for ever. His sense of shame was private and personal, and knew no bounds. What he felt in those moments – and for days (perhaps, for all we know, for the rest of his life) – could never have been adequately described.

If you have fallen and expect to be used by God again, there must be a combination of both *metanoia* (change of mind) and *metamelomai* (remorse). It must also be an irrevocable, no-turning-back state of the mind and will.

Whoever you are, I can promise this: God hasn't finished with you yet. I don't know all that this means for every reader, but, after all, God is no respecter of persons and he loves you as much as he loved Simon Peter.

Final thoughts on Peter

Peter wasn't perfect after his restoration. Acts 10 reveals that he had deep theological and cultural biases that had to be cleansed and dealt with. Until Peter saw God deal with Cornelius, he thought Jews were a cut above everybody else and that a Gentile had to become a Jew before he could be truly converted (verses 34–35, 47). Almost certainly, you and I have a lot of theological baggage left that needs to be cleansed and dealt with too – I can almost guarantee it. I pray to discover my own as soon as possible. But I will need, when I get to heaven, a final discovery and thorough working over of all I have believed and preached that was not totally sound. (Hopefully I can learn some of these things *before* reaching heaven!)

Paul let us in on a rather unpleasant aspect of Peter – at least once. Paul had to chide Peter for abruptly excusing himself from Gentiles when he saw Jews coming along! This is *terrible*! He didn't want fellow Jews to see him being friendly to Gentiles! 'I opposed him to his face,' said Paul, 'because he was clearly in the wrong.' Peter had actually been intimidated by Judaisers (Gal. 2:11–13) – Jews who professed faith in Jesus, but who might not in fact have been converted. So Peter was far from perfect, even after he had been greatly used of God.

When Saul of Tarsus became the Apostle Paul, I can guarantee you that this was not warmly welcomed by many of the Jews who had already embraced Jesus as their God and Messiah. I look forward to watching a video replay of so many things when we get to heaven! But 'all's well that ends well'. Peter granted in the end that Paul's writings, though 'hard to understand', were to be recognised as

Scripture (2 Pet. 3:16). Peter accepted Paul – but only just!

Finally, God did a wonderfully gracious thing for Peter. He gave him a second chance. It came when Peter and John were summoned before the Sanhedrin. They were flogged and then ordered not to speak in the name of Jesus (Acts 5:40). I can imagine how some in the Sanhedrin must have been thinking. 'We showed them, this will teach them a lesson, they have been punished and humiliated. We won't have to be bothered with them again. They are now sorry for what they have done' – or words along these lines.

The truth is, Peter and John were so excited and thrilled to be blessed in this way that they had to pinch themselves to believe it. Whereas most people I know dread any kind of shame or humiliation, all I know is that Peter and John left the Sanhedrin, 'rejoicing because they had been counted worthy of suffering disgrace for the Name' (Acts 5:41). Think about that phrase: 'counted worthy'. Who counted them 'worthy'? Answer: God. What a privilege it was to be 'counted worthy' to suffer shame for Jesus! That is exactly the way they felt. It was Peter's second chance. He was so grateful that he had been given a second chance to stand up for the name – and that he hadn't blown it this time. God is so gracious.

If God can use Peter – with all his weaknesses and biases – he can use you and me.

Conclusion

I suppose every author likes to think that his or her latest book is their 'best yet'. I also suspect, if they are Christian writers, they like to think every word they have written has been inspired. One of my publishers told me of one of their authors who refused to let an editor tamper with his material because 'God wrote it'.

I can assure you, God did not write this book! I did. I certainly do not hold God responsible for the material in this book! If I were to say how little or how much I felt 'helped', I would possibly be crossing over a line. I can say with certainty only that I *asked* God a lot for his help. I wrote it from my heart and experience – which goes back well over fifty years.

As I close, I want to make six final suggestions:

1 *Let God decide whether you will be used again.* We can all come up with our formulas and recipes for

restoration, but at the end of the day it is up to God who is restored, reinstated and given a second chance to engage in ministry or trusted positions. I think that he decides on a case-by-case basis, so be willing to wait at the end of the queue. Wait until your name is called.

2 *Wait until you are asked to return.* When you were first called to do God's work, did you not receive an invitation? When God comes to a person a second time, he who *recommences* a good work will complete it (cf. Phil. 1:6). Wait for the invitation, however long it takes. If it never comes, can you leave things in God's hands? My loving counsel is this: don't rush things, don't manipulate. Don't promote yourself. 'No-one from the east or the west or from the desert can exalt a man. But it is God who judges: he brings one down, he exalts another' (Ps. 75:6–7).

3 *Value your own personal relationship with God above a public role.* At the Judgement Seat of Christ, about which this book has had a lot to say, it will be your personal relationship with God that will matter most. Esteem this above anything else. If getting into the ministry or a position of authority in the Church means more to you than becoming more like Jesus and knowing him, I would have to say to you in all candour: you are not ready yet.

4 *If someone comes to you, saying categorically that God will not use you again, you have a right to ask by what*

authority they are making such a pronouncement. I hope I am not being unfair, but such a position smacks of a pharisaical interpretation of Scripture – not one that mirrors a God of tenderness towards bruised reeds. I also cannot help but ask, how might that person's position change if *he or she*, or a loved one, should in the future fall into the very trap they have condemned?

It would seem that God is more gracious than some of us.

What I *do* know is that God has chosen to fill up the Bible with all kinds of shady, broken, failed people who exemplify his amazing willingness to receive them back when, like the prodigal son, they 'come to themselves'.

5 *Whether God offers to restore and reinstate you or not, begin now to devote the rest of your life to building a superstructure of gold, silver and precious stones.* This means a life of sexual purity, transparent integrity and genuine meekness, a heart devoid of bitterness, and a will not bent on vindication.

6 *If by the grace of God you are restored, avoid a self-righteous spirit.* Never judge those who led to your exposure and be sympathetic to Christians who are slow to accept you.

May the blessing of the Triune God – Father, Son and Holy Spirit – be upon you for the rest of your life. Amen.

Totally
Forgiving
Ourselves

R. T. KENDALL

Turn over for the first chapter of
another inspirational book by R. T. . . . .

HODDER

1

Ten Reasons Why We Should Totally Forgive Ourselves

There is no fear in love. But perfect love drives
out fear because fear has to do with
punishment. The one who fears is not made
perfect in love. (1 John 4:18)

God does not oppress us.
Dr Martyn Lloyd-Jones

Have you ever felt guilty at the thought of totally forgiving yourself? I have.

The idea is this. What I have done is so horrible that I *do not deserve* to be set free from guilt. It would be irresponsible to forgive myself totally and not look back. I must pay for my failure. I must see that I get justice.

The same is true in forgiving others. We are afraid they will not get justice. To forgive them sets them free and therefore means they may not get punished. When my friend Josef Tson said to me, 'RT, you must totally forgive them', I was not happy. Josef recalls how angry I was at his suggestion! But I knew he was right. I eventually took his advice and was set free with a peace I had forgotten about. The old peace I knew many years before returned. It was absolutely fantastic!

But some weeks later I began to think about what I had done. I had set them free. This meant that they were totally off the hook. They would never get found out. This was not fair. People should know! They have got away with it! And a feeling of anger welled up inside me. The peace left. I was back to square one.

So I forgave them again. However, not by going to them – that would have been totally counterproductive. I knew they would not think they had done anything wrong in the first place. It is an important rule: *never tell a person you have forgiven them unless they are sincerely asking for it*. Like it or not, 90 per cent of the people we have to forgive probably do not think they have done anything wrong. So don't expect to sort things out with the one who has hurt you. I therefore never approached them. The total forgiveness was in *my heart*. That is where the peace is. When I forgave them again, the peace returned with it!

But months later I began to ponder yet again on what they had done to us. How dare they do this! How dare they think like that! What is more, *nobody* will ever know. They are not getting justice – they are totally free. And –

surprise, surprise – the peace vanished again.

I have to tell you, I went back and forth, back and forth, for months. The peace would come and go in direct proportion to my attitude towards those who had hurt Louise and me.

I'm sorry it took a while, but I came to a conclusion: *the peace is better!*

The way forward is to set such a high value on the *peace you get* from total forgiveness that you prefer the peace more than their being punished. Live by this rule: *peace is better than punishment.*

Further clarification regarding forgiving ourselves

Before we proceed, I must clarify further what the implications are when we totally forgive ourselves: it is not only letting ourselves off the hook but also setting ourselves free from any sense of punishment. This includes accepting ourselves as we are and never looking back. It is letting the past be past. Paul the apostle had on his conscience that he had persecuted, even tortured, Christians (Phil. 3:6; Acts 22:4–6, 26:10–11) but went on to say, 'This one thing I do: *forgetting what is behind* and straining towards what is ahead, I press on towards the goal to win the prize for which God has called me heavenward in Christ Jesus' (Phil. 3:13–14). Paul not only knew he was forgiven; he had forgiven himself.

John said that perfect love casts out fear and that 'fear has to do with punishment' (1 John 4:18). The Authorized Version says 'fear hath torment'. This is true of course, but that is not exactly what John actually said in 1 John 4:18. Fear *kolasiv echei* – 'has, or possesses, punishment'. The person living in fear is obsessed with the idea of punishment. This means at least four things: (1) that the person who lives in fear is already punished by this fear, truly living in torment; (2) the person is in fear of being punished by God; (3) the person in fear is always punishing himself or herself; and (4) the person who lives in fear always wants to punish others.

Various translations bring out some of these meanings. 'If we are afraid, it is for fear of what he [God] might do to us' (Living Bible). 'Fully developed love expels every particle of fear, for fear always contains some of the torture of feeling guilty' (Phillips Modern English). 'To fear is to expect punishment' (Jerusalem Bible).

Fear is in a sense its own punishment. In much the same way that love is its own reward, which means it is fulfilling in itself, so too fear is tormenting. When one lives in fear, we often feel they we are being punished by God all the time. If that is not enough, we do it to ourselves – we beat ourselves black and blue for our past sins. If that too is not enough, we almost always take it out on others. In other words, we fear that justice isn't going to be carried out on those who have been unjust to us. We move in on God's territory because we are fearful that they won't get what's coming to them. Never mind that God said, 'It is mine to avenge' (Heb. 10:30); we get impatient with the way he seems not to avenge them. So we try to do it for him.

All this is traceable to fear. God has not given us a spirit of fear (2 Tim. 1:7). Dr Lloyd-Jones used to say, 'God never oppresses us'. When we feel oppressed, we should realise straightaway that this oppression did not come from God.

So here is what we too often do: we punish ourselves for what we have done. 'I deserve to feel guilty. It would be quite wrong for me to feel good. What I did was bad. I cannot live with what I have done (or should have done but didn't). I deserve some kind of punishment.' In the same way, when it comes to forgiving others, we recall what they did. We say, 'They deserve to feel guilty. It is quite wrong for them to feel good. What they did was bad. They deserve punishment.' So we punish them – whether by telling others what they did or making sure they feel guilty over what they did.

Not forgiving ourselves, then, is often an unconscious effort to punish ourselves. We often don't realise that is what we are doing. In the same way that we get angry if others do not get the justice they deserve – and we step in and punish them, so we ourselves feel that we are not getting the justice we deserve (by our regrettable past), so we punish ourselves.

We therefore punish ourselves by not forgiving ourselves. We would feel guilty if we forgave ourselves! We should not let ourselves off the hook! And the thought of *totally* forgiving ourselves would be utterly unfair! Besides, what right do I have to take authority and forgive myself? This book will answer that question.

Why you should forgive yourself

Why should we forgive ourselves?

First, *it is precisely what God wants you to do*. This is what many of us have difficulty in believing. There are various reasons for this, such as a misunderstanding of the nature of God, not to mention a faulty perception of the gospel of Jesus Christ. It seems too good to be true that God would totally forgive us all our sins because Jesus died on the cross for us.

If you are not convinced that God wants you to forgive yourself, I hope you will be convinced by the end of this book.

It is a sin against God not to forgive ourselves. Why? Because in precisely the same way that it is a sin to be bitter, to hold a grudge and not to forgive others (Eph. 4:31–32), so it is a sin to be bitter towards ourselves, hold a grudge against ourselves and not to forgive ourselves. We forgive in proportion to how we love; we withhold forgiveness in proportion to how we hate. God did not create us to hate ourselves. The most natural thing in the world is to love ourselves. This was an assumption in the command that we love our neighbour as we love ourselves (Matt. 19:19).

In the meantime, consider these words of Jesus. The opening words of the Sermon on the Mount are: 'Blessed are the poor in spirit, for theirs is the kingdom of heaven. Blessed are they that mourn, for they shall be comforted' (Matt. 5:3–4). I am *not* saying that not forgiving yourself is always the same thing as being poor in spirit or mourning. But the spirit of tenderness from God implied in these words nonetheless is an invitation to those who feel guilty about their past. It is an invitation to look carefully at these words and see what they *do* mean.

What do they mean? Being poor in spirit means you realise you have no bargaining power with God, that you realise you are spiritually bankrupt. If you feel this way about your sin, then take it as a hint that God wants you be encouraged, that you do acknowledge your sin but also move on. God can use your past failure to get your attention in order that you inherit the kingdom of heaven. The very thing that haunts you most could turn out to be the best thing that ever happened to you.

The next word says that those who mourn will be comforted. This mourning refers primarily to conviction of sin, and you should see your past failure as traceable to sin. Unless your problem is one of pseudo-guilt, which I will deal with in the next chapter, then acknowledge your sins before the Lord. Jesus welcomes sinners (Luke 15:2). Furthermore, Jesus always reaches out to *anybody* who mourns – as in the case when he said to the widow who was burying her only son, 'Don't cry' (Luke 7:13). God does not want you to punish yourself for your past. As we will see more clearly later on, God punished *Jesus* for your failure. He will not comfort you in your mourning as long as you are trying to atone for your past by punishing yourself. And what is the promise to those who mourn? 'They shall be comforted' (Matt. 5:4). What else could that mean in your case but having the grace to accept God's forgiveness and totally forgive yourself?

I only know that it is said of Jesus, 'A bruised reed he will not break' (Matt. 12:20). That is what you are – a bruised reed. When you are bruised, you are poor in spirit. God is calling you to accept his total forgiveness and comforts you with grace to forgive yourself. When you are bruised, be sure that God is not going to rip you to shreds. He is not going to shame you, moralise you and say 'you do not feel guilty enough you wretched creature'. It gives our Lord pain that you are in misery. He is *touched* – not repelled – by your weakness (Heb. 4:15, AV). He invites you at this moment to forgive yourself – totally.

Jesus was given a mandate to 'release the oppressed' (Luke 4:18). There is nothing more oppressive than guilt. God does not oppress us and is not the author of fear. Fear is of the devil. The devil wants you to be afraid and he certainly *does not want you to forgive yourself*. This brings us to the next reason why you should forgive yourself.

Second, *Satan does not want you to forgive yourself*. I have believed for a long time that one of the ways to know the will of God is to imagine what the devil would want you to do – then do the opposite. When I can surmise (and most of us have a fairly shrewd idea what the devil would want us to do) what Satan would like, I am halfway to knowing what God wants. Do the opposite of what you know the devil wants you to do and you will be on safe territory. You need more information than that, of course; you need to know your Bible so well that you don't have to guess what God's will is (Eph. 5:17). But if you can figure out what the devil would want you to do, good; that means you should do the opposite and you will be moving in the right direction.

For example, what do you think the devil would want you to do regarding having sex outside marriage? Be honest! You *know* that Satan would say, 'Do it, go for it, God made you to have sexual fulfilment.' The devil always wants what is against God's word – the Bible. The Bible has made it clear that sex outside marriage is sin. I'm sorry, but there is no grey area here. When you therefore know what the devil would want you to do regarding sex outside marriage, but you remain chaste and pure, you know you have honoured God.

The devil would *not* want you to pray and read your Bible. So what should you do? You pray and read your Bible all the more! I could go on and on. But I am counting on you to know what I mean by now.

So, regarding forgiveness, what do you suppose the devil wants? In 2 Corinthians 2:10–11, Paul said, 'I have forgiven in the sight of Christ for your sake, in order that Satan might not outwit us. For we are not unaware of his schemes.' I love the Living Bible's translation: 'A further reason for forgiveness is to keep from being outsmarted by Satan; for we know what he is trying to do.'

Why would Paul refer to forgiveness in connection with the devil's schemes? The answer is very sobering: because *our lack of total forgiveness is an open invitation for the devil to move in*. In other words, when I do not totally forgive those who have hurt me, I have said to the devil, 'Come and get me, do what you want with me.' This is scary. I certainly don't want to do that. But Satan is crafty and is lurking around us day and night, looking for an entry. When he finds us holding a grudge he exploits it to the full. He knows that as long as I do not totally forgive, the Holy Spirit – the heavenly dove – will fly away for a season. God cannot use me to the full when I am carrying a grudge.

So too, then, with forgiving ourselves. Satan does not want you to forgive yourself. He loves your misery. Your bondage makes him happy. You are no threat to him or his interests when you are punishing yourself, fearing God's wrath, living in torment over what happened yesterday – or years ago. By the way, the devil knows what happened in your past too. He has been around thousands of years and got on your case the moment you sided with his arch-enemy Jesus Christ. He will exploit your past to the hilt. His design: to keep you paralysed and living in a pit of near despair over what is in the past.

Would you not agree, then, that a good reason to forgive yourself is because it is the opposite of what the devil wants for you? Since you know that what he wants is for you not to forgive yourself, then do the opposite. I pray that in this moment you will begin to forgive yourself – totally.

Third, *you will have inner peace and freedom from the bondage of guilt.* There is nothing to compare with the peace and freedom that comes from total forgiveness. 'Where the Spirit of the Lord is, there is freedom' (2 Cor. 3:17).

I have told many times about my 'Damascus Road experience' when driving in my car on 31 October 1955. It was not my conversion, however; it came a few years after my conversion. My point in mentioning this is that I was given the most wonderful peace, joy, rest of soul and assurance on that day. It was incredibly brilliant. But about ten months later I lost the peace I had – for some reason. I tried every way under the sun to get it back. I started praying for two hours every morning (like John Wesley). It did me no harm, but I didn't get the peace back. I started tithing. It did me no harm, but I didn't get the peace back. I started double tithing (for a while). It did me no harm, but I didn't get the peace back. I would ask any godly person to lay hands on me for a greater anointing. All these things no doubt helped me in my spiritual growth.

But when I took Josef Tson's words seriously, applying them by totally forgiving those who hurt me, I was amazed! The old peace returned!

God will do this for you too. He is no respecter of persons. He beckons you as you read these lines to enjoy total forgiveness.

That includes forgiving yourself.

You will perhaps ask whether I have had an equivalent experience in totally forgiving myself as I did in forgiving others? The answer is, yes, but it was not an exact equivalent experience. But almost. The peace that came to me from forgiving myself – being set free from guilt over being a father that was too busy – came in waves and stages. It has not been so dramatic but it has been equally satisfying. And, believe me, this satisfaction has been just as important and fulfilling as the peace that came to me from forgiving others. I say that because the enormity of the guilt I felt was so awful that I needed help! God brought me through this. Otherwise I could not write this book.

You too should forgive yourself because of the peace and freedom that awaits you. Nobody knows better than I how it feels when the devil reminds you of your past and your shortcomings. The feeling is horrible.

Are you weighted down with guilt over the past? It does not need to last. I am hoping that in these lines you are moving towards the internal victory and peace that awaits you. There is light at the end of the tunnel! Your emancipation could come in one of two ways: either you could have a sudden experience by the grace of the Holy Spirit that sets you free; or you may, like myself, come into this in increments. Either way is just as valid, for when you realise you have forgiven yourself the result is inner peace.

Fourth, you should forgive yourself because *the degree to which you forgive yourself may directly relate to your usefulness*. When I find myself wallowing in self-pity I am of little use to my work. Not forgiving myself is paralysing.

This is the way it was with King David. We will take a closer look at him later, but I am referring now to how he grieved over his son Absalom's tragic death. David knew all too well that what happened to his son had actually begun with David's own sin and folly. But his mourning for Absalom went too far – and he almost had another crisis on his hands. His servant Joab warned him to snap out of this grief and self-pity at once – or his followers would desert him. David immediately took Joab's advice (2 Sam. 19:1–8). Not forgiving yourself is immobilising – it diminishes your usefulness.

Most of my ministry has been preparing sermons and preaching. It is impossible to say which I enjoy more – preaching or preparation. But with either of these, I am utterly dependent upon the anointing of the Spirit. If the anointing is there, preparation comes easily; so too with the preaching. But the absence of the anointing means that I can struggle for hours and days in preparation. Why? No insights come. I live for insight – that is my calling. But insight comes in direct proportion to the anointing, and the anointing comes in direct proportion to my relationship with the Holy Spirit.

In a word: when I grieve the Holy Spirit, insights are

nowhere around. My own style has been not to read commentaries and books in preparation unless I am completely flummoxed – then I turn to others. What thrills me most of all is when the Spirit enables me to see things in the Bible without the aid of other writers. When the anointing is on me in preparation, insights come. When the anointing lifts, I might as well try to fly to the moon.

Therefore when I am preoccupied with my failures of the past, I lose heart. I cannot get anywhere in preparing a sermon or writing a book. I am helpless. Therefore I have learned that it is in my own interest to forgive myself totally – and not listen to Satan's accusations! The only way forward for me has been to disregard every single suggestion of the devil that would bring me down! In other words, I can tell you that totally forgiving others and totally forgiving myself has been my lifeline to the anointing of the Spirit.

Whatever your own gift and calling is, I dare say you are in the same situation. You will struggle in your life and calling when you are weighed down with guilt. Guilt and usefulness don't get on well with each other! Therefore I would urge you to accept the thesis of this book if only for this reason: your usefulness will be impaired as long as you are crippled internally by guilt from your past. Don't deprive the Holy Spirit of the pleasure he gets by using you to the full!

I knew a doctor in Florida who drank heavily in order to

work through the pain of his past. What was so sad was that he would leave his patients waiting. He would get drunk and not be able to come to work. He eventually lost his practice. This is perhaps an extreme example of how guilt keeps one from being useful, but let me caution you, should you need it: alcohol will not make the past go away. Totally forgiving yourself must be done soberly, consciously and voluntarily. Just as in the case of forgiving others, totally forgiving yourself is an act of the will. But it leads to your being at your best.

Fifth, totally forgiving yourself *will help you love people more*. The reason you do not forgive yourself totally is very possibly because you do not like yourself. Some people think it is an admirable thing to say, 'I hate myself'. I must lovingly tell you, that it is an abominable thing to say. Do you honestly think that God wants you to hate yourself? Do you think he made you to hate yourself? Why ever did our heavenly Father tell us that we should love God with all our hearts but also to love your neighbour *as you do yourself* (Matt. 19:19)? I must say it again, these words carry with them an implicit assumption that we love ourselves. It is normal to love yourself. You were created that way. It is sin that brings about self-hatred.

People who do not totally forgive those who hurt them often do not like themselves. It is not surprising, then, that they struggle with liking people. So too with forgiving yourself. When you totally forgive yourself, your perception not only of yourself but others changes. They aren't so bad after all! What is more, you begin more and more to care for others – and to love them.

The fringe benefits that come from forgiving yourself are vast. And one of them is: you find it easier to love people. I do not say that forgiving yourself will make you a Mother Theresa, but you may well be surprised how much easier it is to get involved in other people's problems and worries. But when you and I are so preoccupied with ourselves, we somehow never get around to caring for others, much less loving them. Forgiving ourselves is emancipating. You begin to love yourself as God intends, and you find it easier to care for others.

Neither does this mean that you will become an extrovert. You can in any case be an extrovert and not care about others. But there is an inner freeing of oneself that enables you to be concerned about other people. We are not speaking therefore of a personality change, but I am saying that forgiving yourself will enable you to stop focusing only on yourself and focus also on others. You are never – ever – asked not to care about your own needs. What Paul said is this: 'Each of you should look not only to your own interests, but *also* to the interests of others' (Phil. 2:4). It was at that point Paul embarked upon one of the most sublime passages in all Holy Writ – which was all about becoming more like Jesus (Phil. 2:5–11).

Jesus did not hate himself. He was sinless, of course, and we are not expected to become entirely like him in this life (that awaits our glorification, 1 John 3:3). But I am saying that totally forgiving ourselves will help us to love people 'more' than before. For when we have not forgiven ourselves we are not in a position even to think about loving others because we are consumed with ourselves.

Sixth, *people will like you more when you have forgiven yourself.* Of course you want to be liked! The person who says 'I don't care what they think', when it comes to the human need of affirmation, almost certainly has a severe personality handicap. We all want to be liked. It is human to want friends. Dale Carnegie wrote a bestseller that sold millions, his book *How to Win Friends and Influence People.* So much of what he taught is embedded in the book of Proverbs. He was quite biblical without knowing it. But you can read that book, and even profit from it, and find that it may not make people like you – when you are riddled with guilt. The thing is, when you totally forgive others and yourself, much of what Dale Carnegie taught might be exemplified in you without your having read his book!

'A man that hath friends must shew himself friendly' (Prov. 18:24, AV). Do you want people to like you? Be friendly! But it is so hard to do this when we are bedevilled with our own personal problems.

When I was pastor in Fort Lauderdale, we had a woman who came to our church who said that our people were so unfriendly. I alerted some of the members there and urged them to go out of their way to be nice to this woman. They tried, but noticed that she always left the service during the last hymn – and went and sat in her car all by herself until her husband came out. She never gave the people a chance! The problem was she was consumed with herself.

I don't mean to be unfair, but not forgiving yourself is a selfish thing. I'm sorry, but it is. It is an exhibition of the wrong kind of self-love. There is a difference between loving yourself and self-love. It is not a play on words. Self-love is preoccupation with your personal desires and concerns; loving yourself is respecting yourself as God intends.

In a word: forgiving yourself makes you more likeable. People will want to be near you. They will feel that you care about them.

My friend Lyndon Bowring has more close friends than anybody I have ever met. I know a dozen (I am one of them) who regard him as their best friend. Why? I happen to know. Lyndon is one of the few persons I have become acquainted with who doesn't focus on himself but on those who seek him out. Everybody seems to want to be near him. He not only tolerates listening to people, he loves them! And they love him.

The place to begin, if you have a problem with people not liking you, is to forgive yourself – totally.

Seventh, the reason you should forgive yourself is because *it will enable you to fulfil all God has in mind for you and thus keep you from being paralysed by the past.* The gifts and calling of God are without repentance – which means that they are 'irrevocable' (Rom. 11:29). You cannot lose them. Even King Saul, in his disobedience and pursuit of David (hoping to kill him) still prophesied with the same gift God gave him some time before (1 Sam. 10:9–11, 19:23–24). This is proof enough that having certain gifts, however beneficial, does not require that we are walking with the Lord.

Paul refers to various gifts of the Spirit in 1 Corinthians 12:8–10. He then discusses different levels of service and profile one may have in the church – as being the foot, the hand, the eye, the ear, etc. (1 Cor. 12:14–29). But he shows that these gifts are worthless to the body of Christ if we do not have love (1 Cor. 13). Part of love is not pointing the finger; in other words, keeping no record of wrongs (1 Cor. 13:5).

Forgiving yourself is refusing to point the finger at yourself in a way that keeps you feeling guilty. Love keeps no record of other people's wrongs and, when forgiving ourselves, it keeps no record of our own wrongs. Not that we can ever forget our past – no. Neither do we forget what others have done to us; it is just that we do not bring these things up. So, in the same way, we must not bring things up to ourselves. We refuse to think about them, refuse to dwell on them.

When you have totally forgiven yourself, it brings considerable confidence. Consider Simon Peter. He denied that he even knew Jesus to a Galilean servant girl. This is because the authorities were watching. Peter was in utter fear before them. But when the rooster crowed and Jesus looked at him, Peter knew he was found out and wept bitterly (Matt. 26:69–75). Some seven weeks later Peter addressed thousands on the Day of Pentecost with a fearlessness and confidence that baffled everyone (Acts 2). How was this possible? Peter was totally forgiven and totally forgave himself.

When we cannot forgive ourselves it is hard to look at people in the eyes. It is hard not to look down. We feel guilty, look guilty.

God wants to use those who are free of guilt – totally forgiven. But that forgiveness is of little value on our psychological frame when we do not truly *believe* we have been forgiven. When we truly believe we have been forgiven, it shows. When we have totally forgiven ourselves, it shows. God can use us. People will want what we have.

Eighth, *your own physical health could be at stake*. In *Total Forgiveness* I referred to non-Christian organisations on both sides of the Atlantic that have been set up to help people to forgive. They are not doing it with the teachings of the Bible in mind. They are doing it for other reasons: one's health and well-being.

It has been proved by medical research that holding a grudge can injure your health. Studies have revealed that un-forgiveness can lead to high blood pressure, heart disease, kidney disease, arthritis and other ailments. I don't want *you* to think that, if you have any of these problems, this is the reason. But with some people this is the case.

So if non-Christian organisations can be formed to help

people overcome grudges without using the Bible, surely those who believe the Bible should take the lead!

It is reasonable to assume, then, that if anger and bitterness are injurious to your physical health, not forgiving yourself is bad for your health too. This is because you are holding a grudge against yourself!

In the Lord's Prayer Jesus put our physical needs before the spiritual. First came 'give us this day our daily bread'; then came 'forgive us our trespasses as we forgive those who trespassed against us' (see Matt. 6:9–13; Luke 11:2–4). Why did Jesus put the physical before the spiritual? It is because we have to eat in order to live. God gave us bodies. He is looking after us in the Lord's Prayer. Furthermore, our daily bread does not only mean food; it means the essentials of life – shelter and clothing as well.

This means God cares about our health. We must take care of our bodies. They are temples of the Holy Spirit (1 Cor. 6:19). When forgiving ourselves is related to one's health, that is a fairly substantial reason to take this matter seriously!

Ninth, because *our mental and emotional health could be at stake*. The main problem all counsellors face – whether their clients have a religious background or not – is that of *guilt*. Guilt may well be a theological matter, but it is a psychological one as well. There is not a psychiatrist or psychologist on the planet who does not deal with this in their sessions every day.

Guilt is crippling – affecting not only our bodies but also

our minds and emotions. The degree to which we cope with guilt will be the degree to which we have good mental health. Dr Frederick Perls, who was a humanistic psychologist, used to say that he could heal any psychopathology in one hour if he could get his client not to feel guilty.

Sometimes people in the world scoff at us in the Church when we behave like neurotics and not solidly mature men and women. Where we currently attend church the pastor Steve Vetter has put this word in his weekly bulletin: 'Key Largo Baptist Church Family is a group of imperfect people who have been brought together by the grace of God to worship Him'. This is very true and helpful. We should nonetheless make every effort to deal with bad habits, wrong attitudes and even emotional problems that militate against a good Christian testimony. It pleases God for his people to have good mental health. Forgiving ourselves is a good place to begin.

Finally, we should forgive ourselves because *our spiritual state is at stake*. There is an inseparable connection between our spiritual health and a good relationship with the Holy Spirit. The Holy Spirit is *in* every Christian (Rom. 8:9), but not necessarily *un-grieved* in every Christian.

The Holy Spirit is a person – a very sensitive person at that. He can be grieved. 'Do not grieve the Holy Spirit of God, with whom you were sealed for the day of redemption' (Eph. 4:30). The word 'grieve' comes from a Greek word that can mean to get your feelings hurt. The Holy Spirit can get his feelings hurt! How? By our bitterness and grudges. The next thing Paul said was: 'Get rid of all bitterness, rage and anger, brawling and slander, along with every form of malice. Be kind and compassionate to one another, forgiving each other, just as in Christ God forgave you' (Eph. 4:31–32).

When we are filled with anger and bitterness, the Holy Spirit is grieved. This does not mean we have lost our salvation. Paul said we are 'sealed for the day of redemption' – nothing can be clearer than that! But when the Spirit is grieved, as when the heavenly dove lifts from us, we are left to ourselves. It is because of a temporary lifting of the anointing of the Holy Spirit. The result is that we are irritable, have no presence of mind, cannot think clearly and have little or no insight as to the next step forward.

It all comes down to this matter of total forgiveness.

Therefore we must totally forgive ourselves if we want the heavenly dove to rest on us – and enjoy the fruits of the Spirit such as love, joy, peace, longsuffering, gentleness, etc. (Gal. 5:22–23). Forgiving ourselves helps ensure that the anointing is on us; not doing so means that we forfeit a measure of his presence.

Temporarily losing a sense of God's presence does not need to happen. It should not happen. But it does happen. I have grieved the Spirit so many times that I would die a thousand deaths if you could see a video replay of my whole life. But you won't. Because God has forgiven my sins. The blood of Jesus has washed them all away. And the least I can do, therefore, in the light of God forgiving me is to forgive myself.

That is what he wants of you and me. Totally forgiving ourselves is not merely an option; we have a command from God to do this. With this mandate accepted by us, God can use us to exceed all we ever dreamed of.

He will use *you* to an extent you never thought possible. If God can forgive and use a man who knew Jesus intimately as Peter did – and who fell pitifully and horribly, he can use you and me. Jesus never stopped loving Peter. Knowing in advance that Peter would deny him, Jesus even said to him, 'I have prayed for you, Simon, that your faith may not fail. And when you have turned back, strengthen your brothers' (Luke 22:32).

Peter had Jesus' prayers behind him. So do we. Jesus' prayer for Peter enabled him to forgive himself. His prayer will do that for you too.